As Love Wrinkles

D1267734

Ann Preston & Louise Cowan

outskirts
press

Lovingly dedicated to our mothers

We are not professionals. The opinions expressed in this manuscript simply share our own stories of love, commitment, and faith as we cared for our aging mothers.

Table of Contents

Chapter 1: The Why   1

Chapter 2: How We Met; Plan Or Coincidence   11

Chapter 3: Meet Catherine   17

Chapter 4: Meet Martha   23

Chapter 5: Catherine's Maze Of Gray   27

Chapter 6: Navigating In The Fog   57

Chapter 7: What We've Learned   79

Chapter 8: Healing – *It Was Never Personal*   85

Chapter 9: Faith, The Ultimate Healer   91

CHAPTER 1

The Why

This is the true story of two women, unrelated to one another and caring for aging mothers and the shocking realities that accompany that phase of life, a phase of life that is so individualized it defies a specific definition. It is a story of love, commitment, and faith tested until the last breath and longer. We say longer, because it took years for our hearts to heal from our inner conflict.

We share two different stories, yet the experiences and feelings we faced are similar. It is a true testament to our parents for making us the women we are. We are women whose families come first, not because they had to, but because we wanted them to. Our mothers gave us and instilled a love inside us to endure, even when we wanted to give up or were on the verge of collapsing from exhaustion. The most difficult times show the strength of love. We were taught to have an open and understanding heart and mind to all we meet. It does not matter the package a person comes in; what matters is the heart and soul inside that human package. We both are blessed with that love now from our families and a potpourri of loving friends who were always there for us.

For ten years Catherine lived with her daughter Louise and her family, and for five years Martha lived with her daughter Ann. For the first few years of Catherine's living with Louise, it was a humorous blending of three generations; however, both in the case of Catherine and Martha their last few years of living with their daughters were a true test of love, commitment, and patience for everyone.

Thousands of baby boomers are facing the responsibility of parenting parents. Many others are caring for children and adults suffering from illnesses, both physical and mental. Though our story focuses on parenting our aging parents, there are many similarities of committed caregivers.

We love those we care for as much as humanly possible, but at times our patience is stretched as far as it can go. When elderly parents live in the same home as their child, it is a constant, no-break routine with little or no help. We were lost when looking for help, since there didn't seem to be as many support groups available years ago. Without a significant physical diagnosis, one of Alzheimer's or dementia, support services were nearly non-existent. Though there are more today, there is never enough for the 24/7 caregiver who feels trapped inside the lonely world of caregiving. In the middle of caring, cleaning, feeding, nursing duties, dressing, and transporting the parent, there are still the tasks of maintaining their own lives of family and careers. It is hard, my friends, and it took years to admit how hard it really was. One can seek advice and receive some understanding, but so often there is simply no relief. Our parents did not reach a level that ever qualified them for skilled nursing care. It seems as though we are living in a gray world that is making no sense, because it just doesn't make sense.

Our mothers took care of everyone with the strength and love we prayed for, after we took them in. We saw their confusion, but did they? Unfortunately this was the new normal for them as well as us. We, the caregivers, wear down emotionally, sometimes physically, from the stress, and at times our family unit suffers. The day-to-day stress flows over and affects the entire family.

The elderly parent knows something is wrong, but is unable to comprehend it. At this point we simply smile, shake our heads, and just go with the flow. The early wrinkles of the aging process are really no big deal. As the levels of aging progress, dealing with parenting a parent becomes more complicated and overwhelming to us, our families, and most importantly, our mothers.

The one-minute commercials on television are heartwarming, but in the world of the caregiver, life is skewed. We do hold our parent's hands, hug them, kiss them, and try to understand, but the constant demand can be draining, and we begin to hide behind silent smiles. Our mothers want to remain our mothers, and we want to remain their daughters. Unfortunately, these roles suddenly are reversed for us, not by us. We do not have a choice. The mothers we always knew are no longer the mothers we love. They function most days handling the simple daily routines of caring for themselves without supervision, but when asked about some of their poor decisions with medications or finances, they look at us with vacant eyes, as a deer in the headlights. Where are they, and what has happened to them? They seem lost at times, but we too feel lost and afraid. We try to gently monitor some of their actions to protect them, but it becomes clear they resent our gentle intervention, and that loving relationship with our mothers becomes strained, never to be repaired again. It is completely heartbreaking when for your entire life, this precious mother and daughter relationship was the strongest, most perfect and loving.

Growing up and in our young adult life, we agonized over the thought of ever losing our mothers. How would we survive? Our mothers were our rock, our everything. Maybe this is Mother Nature's way of helping us let go. Our love was and always will be as strong as ever, but even the most loving relationships can be damaged by daily frustrations and hurt. Though this hurt was unintentional, it can't help but wear you down. It wasn't personal, but it sure felt that way. After years of constant demand, when death comes, it is as devastating as it is a relief. Each and every tear we cried held a million more tears filled with love.

To all of you unselfish and brave caregivers out there, we hear you, and we sincerely feel what you are feeling, the happiness and the sadness of it all. Most difficult now, looking back, is the guilt we feel of wanting so much to have been even more patient and understanding in our hearts through this difficult process. We wanted to do it perfectly. The guilt we feel is only because we were not perfect, and we so wanted to return the perfect love our mothers gave us. On the outside we were praised by others for being caring and strong. We looked like we were handling it all well, but most days we were crying inside. Our mothers didn't know our hurt. We never wanted them to suspect they were the cause of our pain. For the first time we couldn't share our feelings with each other. We just smiled with silent sadness when we became frustrated or up-set. It truly was a ride on an emotional rollercoaster that did not stop until each of us lost our best friend.

Our story is for all the caregivers, helping them realize it is okay to have the freedom to "feel." Your complete love is what makes this job so difficult, because you care so very much. It seemed as if we were in a constant battle with our own emo-tions. You love, you hate, you hurt, and our hearts feel for all of you. Please remember you will smile again, but after many tears. It will take some years to come to terms with and heal your feelings. The happy memories will shine above the stress-es of caregiving again; we can assure you. Guilt free, maybe not. We both wanted to be perfect at being caregivers, but our emotions got in the way. Those close to us gave us the credit and love to help us see we really did do a wonderful job, even though not perfect. Now that is okay with us, and we want those of you facing this situation to know you are good and will be fine. Keep your faith within you. When all is over, you can lay your head on your pillow at night and rest peacefully, knowing you really did your best taking care of your parents. You were always there for them, for their every need. Unless others have walked in these same shoes, *same* being the key word, they should not criticize, because they do not really know.

We are not medical doctors, social workers, or psychologists, but we must say the gift of support we gave each other and hope to give you can be given only by someone who has figuratively walked in our shoes. Seek physicians, counselors, and professionals to comfort you and give you some guidance. We can share only what we have experienced.

Our story is for a woman who came in flustered to work and teary eyed because of a weekend visit to her mom out of state. It was a four-hour trip, only to be met at the door by her mother who wanted to know why she was there and told her to go home. She was no longer welcome. How could her mother reject and resent the one child who was doing her best to make sure her mom was okay?

It is for a daughter who through necessity takes over her parents' banking, only to discover that they are bouncing checks and risking their financial security. The daughter spoke to the local merchants to make sure any problem was brought to her attention, rather than embarrass her mom.

It is for the daughter of a no-longer-licensed father who hadn't driven in at least twenty years but who defiantly, and secretly, took her car for a leisurely ride and ended up smashing into a brick wall. Luckily, in this case, no one was injured. The only damage was to the brick wall and the car.

It's for a granddaughter taking her grandpa to the grocery store to pick up his weekly groceries, discovering upon returning home that grandpa's pockets were filled with items from the store. When questioned why he took them, his response was "Don't worry; there was plenty left in the store." Good God, he is a thief! Filled with embarrassment, the granddaughter returned the items and tried to explain, and fortunately she was met with much understanding and kindness. Thank you to all out there who just simply say, "I understand." It means the world to us.

Finally, it is for those of you who wake up each morning knowing more than likely the day will be the same. You rise before the sun to steal some alone time, because otherwise there is no alone time. You have raised your children, so you know what demanding days are like.

Caregiving is different and more demanding. You have your tea or coffee and say your morning prayers for more strength, more patience, and more understanding. You want your smile to be sincere without the silence and tears behind it. It will not be the pitter-patter of little footsteps that will start your busy day as when you were younger. You hear sighing, shuffling, and the same conversation you had yesterday, the day before, and the day before that. This part, you will realize as the aging process continues, was the easy part. Again you will smile and politely converse as you always do. You will kiss your mom good-bye as you leave to work or face your normal routine.

When you return, you hug hello, fix your cup of tea, and go up to your bedroom to refocus and take a minute or two for you and your tea. You are ready to resume your next task and converse, like yesterday, as you prepare dinner for your mom and your family. How the evening progresses revolved totally around the type of day Mom had.

As time goes on, not only have your roles changed, but your parent slowly becomes a stronger force in your home. You, the caregiver, in your own home, must care about the needs of your parent, both physically and emotionally, first. We watch as our parents become set in new ways more difficult and challenging to deal with. In your parents' mind you will always be the child, and you should listen to them, and they not to you. It becomes a frustrating relationship because neither will listen to the other. It becomes irrelevant who may be right.

We are sure, and sad, that some of this litany sounds familiar to many. For those outside this world of caregiving, we have seen the heads shaking, eyes rolling, and the comments of "They're old, so just ignore them." However, when behaviors affect others outside the household, it is not so easily ignored. There will always be some who just walk away, pretending it isn't that bad. Those who do not understand will probably never understand. That is okay with us now. We no longer care whether we are being judged. We know we did the right thing, not perfectly, but right.

For those of you inside this world of caring for a parent, if you are like us, we know you can't walk away, so you must deal with it, because you are not made to walk away. Remember you are not alone.

We found our strength through family, friends, and family physicians. It was very hard some days to keep on going and find that strength. What would have helped was someone to take an equal share of the care. There were no days off. Personal days and vacations were not on the itinerary. These days were often used for doctor appointments, helping with post-op recovery, and various other health-care needs. Our families understood, and we thank them and love them even more for their unselfish understanding.

Pats on the back were as unnecessary as pity of any kind. This is what family is. This is what love is all about. We were loved that way and only returned that love.

Again, looking back, we did it, and we really did it well. We did it well because we were perfect in our love, and we would do it all over again.

CHAPTER 2

How We Met;
Plan Or Coincidence

Louise and Ann both are firm believers that there is a master plan, and quite often that plan unfolds in spite of us. It seems the plan was in motion generations prior to our awareness. In hindsight, Louise and Ann can now see how seemingly unconnected things in their lives were already in motion before they met. It is important for you to see how this friendship developed and how far it actually reached. It easily could have been discarded early on.

They both worked at the local school district for many years. It wasn't until a mutual friend and coworker was in the last stages of cancer that they developed their bond.

Each year the school district planned a summer picnic for the twelve-month employees. It gave an opportunity for everyone to socialize and meet coworkers from the entire district. It was nice finally to put a face with the names and voices of coworkers, nice downtime to relax and enjoy.

Denise worked at the district office with Ann and Louise. She was still working but was not up to attending the picnic lunch that summer day. She stayed back at the office. Louise asked Denise what she would like brought back to eat, and Denise said anything would do, especially ice cream. Louise went to the picnic, picked up enough lunch, and of course ice cream, and returned to the office to have lunch with Denise. As Louise walked into the conference room to share lunch, there sat Ann. She decided to stay back and visit with Denise also, so she would not be left alone. Instantly Ann and Louise saw each other's hearts. They were connected; they clicked. Connections with people show how small our world really is and the beauty we discover as the seeds of friendship grow.

Neither Ann nor Louise could have left Denise alone the day of the company picnic. They would not have been able to enjoy one bite of that lunch. Sharing those precious moments with their friend is what fed their souls. Little did they know they were about to share many more of life's moments over the coming years.

Denise had moved to upstate New York from the same metropolitan city Louise grew up in. They discovered that they shared a close friend, Jean, from their hometown also. In conversations between Denise and Louise, they also discovered that their mothers had worked together at the same bank almost forty years earlier.

As time moved on, Ann and Louise said good-bye to their good friend and they were left with their new friendship, without Denise. As the months and years passed, they spent many months walking the same paths. They would meet occasionally for dinner to talk about Denise, work, and family. They met and had the usual "girl talk." They shared stories of the birth of grandchildren and even each of them having the birth of twin grandsons. They spoke of future retirement and many more of life's events, but it was the shared experience of parenting and caring for their moms that solidified their bond.

As retirement approached for both of them, Louise would retire to babysit her grandson and remain in upstate New York. Ann would relocate to western New York to live near her daughter and grandchildren. Ann would bring her mom to live with her. Louise was happy that Ann could make this move and have family support in place as she took on her new responsibility as caregiver. Louise shared some of the interesting adventures she experienced when her mom lived with her for ten years. She shared only some, but not all, of the explicit details, yet. Actually, there was something inside her that thought Ann could handle it better than she herself did, so she gave Ann her blessing and assured her if she ever needed anyone to just talk or vent to, she should never hesitate to call.

Until you truly open your home and life to caring for an elderly parent, it is difficult to understand fully that it is a full-time commitment. Ann was a truly good person with a huge spiritual heart that Louise admired. Louise was religious, but she was still struggling with the feeling of not doing a perfect job as a caregiver. The more Ann talked to Louise, the more they realized their experiences and feelings were more alike than different. Although Louise had not known anyone dealing with this situation while she was still caregiving, it was consoling to now hear it from someone else. As much as it was helpful for Ann to have someone to talk to, it was finally helping Louise heal and understand what she had gone through years before. Finally each had a chance to talk to someone who understood and felt the same.

Ann was a novice at this taking-care-of-mom thing. Louise had already walked in those shoes. She would listen to Ann for hours on the phone as Ann wept her way through this new phase of life; tears of anger, sadness, grief, and guilt. Ann didn't feel like a crazy woman when she talked to Louise. Nothing Ann said shocked Louise; Louise had felt it all. Each phone conversation with Louise gave Ann the strength to keep moving forward, though Ann thought Louise probably collapsed after each conversation, since the calls were at 7:00 a.m. The early hour gave Ann privacy to speak honestly before Martha woke up.

At the time Ann didn't realize the healing and understanding effect it had on Louise. Surprisingly, Louise was being validated by listening to Ann. She may have been the pro and had already gone through caring for and losing her mom, but she needed to hear that she wasn't alone in her thoughts and guilt. Those thoughts and guilt you must realize were not from bad actions or thoughts. It was feelings of frustration, helplessness, and hurt. We never took any feelings of ours out on our moms. We silently put one foot in front of the other and prayed for the grace to make it through another day. Looking back, we are thinking our moms were probably feeling much the same. This new role reversal just didn't seem right to any of us. It was hard, really hard.

The two women spoke often and not only listened to each other but also truly heard each other. There is a difference. Ann was a loving daughter caring for her mom, as Louise had.

Although Louise did not know anyone to talk with while going through the caregiving role, she had her family and two friends, Jean and Penelope, who listened, heard her, and understood.

As Ann and Louise shared their stories, the situation started to make sense to both of them. They had many of the same feelings and emotions, and yes, they were good and caring people. It was normal to feel, just feel. We did care for our parents to the best of our human ability; however, we wanted to feel inside the way we portrayed ourselves on the outside. We did look in control, calm, and caring, but the work was a lot harder than we ever anticipated.

After Ann's mom passed away, the two friends would talk, still often, about their feelings while they cared for their moms and their feelings after their loss. During those talks they realized there were not a lot of resources available that give an honest portrayal of the caregiver's journey through this gray abyss. They both had entered a healing stage, each of them at different points. Louise had lost her mom five years earlier and was slowly healing. As Ann began to heal, it helped Louise find closure.

What became increasingly clear was that they were not the exception to the rule. They have met many women who are in the position of caregiver, and they are open to them about how hard it really is. The look of relief seen on others' faces brought Ann and Louise to this point. If, in their small circle of friends, every woman or man they met shared the same guilt, anger, frustration, and love, then there was a need to get the word out.

You are normal. It is the love and the heart that makes it so hard to look at things objectively and not take caregiving personally, because it isn't personal. It is all part of the process of not only getting through but of letting go, and so Ann and Louise share their stories, one ten years later and the other after a little more than a year.

Our children, who may become our caregivers, need to know this piece of the puzzle of aging. We would like to remain independent as long and as safely as possible. There may come a day when our children will have to help us, care for us, and yes, decide for us. No one wants to give up their independence, but an elderly person's well-being is a priority. This book also has helped validate ourselves.

CHAPTER 3

Meet Catherine

Catherine was raised in an Irish Catholic family. Her parents owned a local tavern, and Catherine worked hard, taking care of the home and chores at the tavern. Her family members were also good customers of their tavern, and Catherine developed a hatred for alcoholic beverages; however, that addiction trait was inside, hidden deep inside until later years. That trait appeared in another form. Catherine grew up during the Depression, and like most people in that era, she learned to work hard and do without any luxuries. Her luxuries were her necessities of life during that time.

She married my dad and had a child at the start of World War II. When Dad, along with Catherine's brother Bill, went to serve overseas during the war, she was left with a toddler and little income, but she possessed the stamina and know-how to work hard and survive. It was tough times for everyone. She would work part-time in a bomb factory during the war and lived very frugally. She would tell stories of walking in the snow to the railroad yard, pulling her toddler in a wagon, or sleigh if the snow was too deep, to get coal scraps for the furnace. She would scoop up used coal, sifting out the ashes, until she got all she could carry to heat the house until the coal ran out. Catherine had to live on less than a little, but Catherine was strong willed and hard working, which was matched only by her strong love of family.

Before the war ended, she received a notice that her brother, Bill, was missing in action. As it turned out, he was captured and in a concentration camp in Germany. When the war ended and prisoners were released, our Uncle Bill was very frail, had lost part of his feet because of suffering frostbite in the concentration camp, and came to live with us until he passed away in 1964. This was the first time I truly became aware of the heartfelt commitment within a loving family. My mom and dad cared for all of us, including Uncle Bill, through sickness and health.

Many years later, as Uncle Bill was struggling with the wrath of cancer, Mom worked full time but hardly missed a visiting hour each day at the hospital or the chance to take him home to be with us, his family. Uncle Bill just wanted to be home with us, and Mom would make sure that happened as often as possible. Mom embraced this responsibility of caring for her brother while working outside the home, raising a family, cooking, cleaning, and giving all of us a home. This was one of my earliest lessons of a true, unselfish caregiver. Those who have ever nursed a cancer patient know what it entails. You are thrown into a gut-wrenching nursing job without training, especially in the early 1960s. At thirteen years old I watched as a kind and gentle man withered away slowly, and in much discomfort. He hurt badly, as we all did, watching this.

My story of looking out for my parents and caring began maybe a bit earlier than some. I watched and took part in helping out with my Uncle Bill, as much as a young girl could. I helped with feeding him and cleaning up for him. He was a gentle man, and we sat and talked as I exercised his arms and legs while he was fighting this awful disease. I wanted so much for him to be strong and well again. I did not realize the outcome of cancer then. My brother, Edward, was eight years older than I and had just graduated college in an Air Force ROTC program and relocated to a base out of state. He was a navigator in the Air Force with hopes of becoming a pilot. Shortly after that, Uncle Bill passed away, which was a heartbreaking loss for all of us.

A few years later in November 1966, when I was a senior in high school, my loving brother was killed in a plane crash while serving in the Air Force. This loss was the breaking point for Catherine, the pillar of our family. She held us together until then. Catherine had a nervous breakdown. Our family of now three was shattered. Who would take care of Dad and me? Dad certainly could not, and I was seventeen. Mom had done almost everything. She worked and took care of everything at home. Dad went to work, but definitely had a drinking problem. Though he never missed work and was meticulous, I depended on Mom for almost everything. It was one of the loneliest times for all of us. Dad lost a son and a wife; Mom lost a son and her strength, and I lost a brother and a mom to a sickness and wondered if Dad would step up or even could. What would become of us?

The tragedies in our lives sometimes make us or break us. This tragedy broke Mom but shocked Dad so much he knew he had to straighten himself out, for himself, but mostly for Mom and me. At that moment, he realized our family was crumbling without the woman responsible for holding it all together, and that stoic caregiver was unable to care for herself or anyone else. Dad then tried alone to deal with his addiction. In those years so much was hidden, and not many sought outside help from professionals, if there even was help so long ago. Dad came through and managed to help himself, maybe not completely, but enough, and that bit of enough was all we needed.

In my senior year in high school when this occurred, I kept busy academically and learned very quickly how to pick up the pieces at home and give some sort of care to my mom and the house and be there for Dad. It was what I had to do, and there was no question. It also became a lonely time for me at home. Our home was silent, as if our family died, and part of it had. My support from home was gone, and I grew up very quickly. There was no time to think of me; there was work to be done, and it wouldn't get done if I curled up in a corner and cried. I had to move forward. This is what my mom would have done, and this is what I learned from her. I was fortunate to have good friends to take my mind off things, and I kept busy with school and extracurricular activities. With help from us and doctors, my mom recovered, or at least she came back to us emotionally; however, I wonder if anyone completely comes back from tragedies like that one. From that time on, though, I felt a responsibility to watch over my parents. For the first time I saw how fragile they were, and I was all they had. Life got back to some normalcy, back to work, back to school. Dad stepped up, and I learned how to step up and care. Mom and Dad taught me well to love and care. When things fell apart, you stepped up. You didn't come first. My family came first, and I liked that.

After marriage and children, I remained very close with my parents. I made sure they were okay and helped with any chores they could not handle. As they aged, my responsibility to care for them grew.

Catherine had been a great role model, caring for our family, our grandfather as he aged—though he did not live with us—and caring for our uncle, who lived with us for probably twenty years, caring for him as he lost his battle with cancer. Mom taught me the complete and unselfish commitment and love for family. This was a lesson I wanted and loved. It was all about family to me also.

This was Catherine: a mother, a wife, and a sister who possessed a heart with room for everyone. I look up to her more now than ever. She was amazing, and even with all her trials, she kept the warmest heart. As my story unfolds, it is important to remember Catherine the way we, our family, remember her. She was the most wonderful mother and an even far greater grandmother. It is important to remember this Catherine, because this was the real Catherine. As she aged, she changed, and now we can remember the real Catherine we loved. We tend to have more patience and understanding with those who have a physical illness that can be seen. Symptoms are clear, and there is usually some sort of treatment. For many of us it is more difficult seeing and understanding the issues that affect the mind as people grow older or have a mental illness of any kind. Their confusion becomes our confusion. Until we come to the realization that we may not see physical symptoms, but mental decline is a real illness displayed differently.

As years passed, my parents' grandchildren were the light of their lives. They brought a special light back into their souls after losing their son. Catherine gave endless love, time, understanding, and humorous stories to each of her grandchildren. There are a million happy memories of Catherine for my children to cherish. It was all about family and how wonderful it was as the family grew. It was heartwarming to see the happiness grandparents and grandchildren can give each other. As a grandparent now, I know it, I feel it, and I love it. I am me because of Catherine. May Catherine's legacy continue with my children and grandchildren.

CHAPTER 4

Meet Martha

Martha was born in the 1920s to parents of little means. At the time of her birth her parents were farmers who were given room and board in exchange for their work on the farm. An opportunity for my grandfather to work for the railroad in the freight house eventually took them from "the country" to a small town in Pennsylvania.

Mom always talked about how she loved to leave the city and go back to the country to spend time with her grandparents. Recently my brother and I decided to investigate this small town and the country she spoke of. We are especially lucky that her ninety-one-year-old brother was our guide, and I began to see and understand my mom more than I ever had.

The country that she loved had truly been wilderness. I was stunned to see how isolated that area was to this day, and my uncle's stories brought to life a part of my mom's life that she never really talked much about. It was a hard life, and I think she wanted to forget. Her dad eventually became a signalman for the railroad and her mom cleaned houses to make ends meet. She grew up with a dad who was home only on the weekends and a mom who worked hard but was a strict disciplinarian and enjoyed a relationship with alcohol. Her mom had also been raised in an orphanage and never received, so couldn't show, unconditional love.

Mom came out of that childhood with a determination to rise above. Mom excelled in loving her children and family. It is because of her that I am the type of person I am today. She taught me that family comes first and that happiness is wanting what you get, not getting what you want.

Her marriage to my father was tumultuous to say the least. She married my dad who had a drinking problem. She raised me and my brother. I admire her ability never to call it quits on her marriage. She stuck it out. Some people would say that it was the wrong thing to do, but she believed you don't bail merely because it's hard.

She was a working mom, but when work was over, she was with family. She was there for all of us always. It never entered her mind to tell family no. She watched grandchildren, took care of her parents as they aged, and was there for my sister-in-law when she was stricken with a brain tumor. She cleaned our houses when our babies were born and cooked delicious meals and even held my father's hand when he died when I was twenty. She modeled commitment with every breath of her being, and I admired her more than anyone I ever knew.

She and I were very close. If she wasn't working, she was with me. We could talk about anything. She was a mom, but she was also my best friend. She learned family commitment through her mother. My grandmother may have enjoyed her alcohol, but she was always there to help family.

I moved away shortly after I was married. I often wonder how she handled that. She never said a word; she just smiled and gave me her blessing, and then she picked herself up by her bootstraps and moved on.

She remarried a wonderful man who loved her and they had ten years together before he passed away suddenly, and once again she was left alone. Once again she picked herself up by her bootstraps and married again. She was sixty-five years old when she started again. My daughter and I always said, "When I grow up I want to be just like her." She and my stepfather had twenty-three great years. For the first time in her life, she was in a position where she was content, happy, and settled and didn't have to be in charge. My stepfather was a caregiver and took over all the things she typically was responsible for, and she was so glad not to have to be the grown up all the time.

I was happy for her, but in hindsight I also realize that she was giving up a lot of the independence that I admired her for, but she was happy, so I was happy. We saw each other one weekend a month and we talked for hours. She would play with my children so I could have a break, and she cooked all our favorite foods. She never met a stepchild that didn't love her. She was our hero.

It was her tenacity, her ability to love and not judge, her faith in God, and her unconditional love that carried us all. She was always there for me. We loved each other's company. Her wish to live with me in her final years and my willingness to say yes came from a bond that I was sure could never be broken, because of what I learned from her about family commitment.

CHAPTER 5

Catherine's Maze Of Gray

Catherine's story was about a mind that slowly became a clouded maze, drifting in and out of gray confusion. It was gray because it really was not a total state of confusion or lack of coherency. There were times of clear thinking that could become unrealistic in a matter of minutes.

We cautiously look on as our aging parents maintain an independent and safe lifestyle. They are quite capable of the normal daily routines. However, as time passed, we observed some of those routines becoming less consistent.

While watching my mom age, it gradually became apparent that there no longer was black or white in her way of thinking, but a gray understanding of things. That understanding was confusion as to what was right or wrong, in some situations. I have also witnessed that some of the traits and personalities of our aging parents mostly remain, at least in my case, through this aging process. I noticed some traits that one may have been able to control during the younger years, when there was a black and white to rational thinking, that seemed to have become stronger or weaker or simply gray and cloudy. The direction the traits would go sometimes depended on the day or sometimes it depended on the situation. The traits and habits that we as adults have the ability to control seemed to falter as mom aged. I began to notice the "pleases," the "thank you's," the holding of doors, and just simple manners that mom had taught me were forgotten by her. The common courtesies began to disappear. Impulsiveness became a habit. Watching the elderly I discovered this behavior was quite common and really not that big a deal. It was certainly not intentional.

As I mentioned earlier, I felt responsible for my parents since the death of my brother. I was all they had. As my life happened, it always included my parents.

My husband had an opportunity to relocate with his company to upstate New York. My husband knew my parents would have to be a part of our move. I was all they had, and I would not leave them behind. Our children had a special closeness to their grandparents that was an important part of their lives and sense of family. My parents were excited about the move and relocating along with us, which was not only important to me, but also to the loving and close relationship they had with our children. My parents followed us upstate less than a year after our relocation. A little more than a year later, my dad had a return of his colon cancer. For the next six months, I worked, raised a family, taught religious education, and spent endless days and nights visiting the hospital with our family. When dad came home, my husband and I alternated nights at my parents' home to care for my dad. My mom could not, at seventy-five years old, drive daily to the hospital, change ileostomy bags, or prepare feeding tubes. Not only was I worried about my dad, but I also realized my mom was crumbling from the pressure. The stress was too much for her, and she became more fragile and dependent upon my husband and me. She became more quiet and uneasy being alone. My husband and I spent many sleepless nights caring for Dad as he battled cancer. Fortunately our home was able to accommodate Mom so she would not have to stay alone in her house when Dad was in the hospital. After six months, Dad passed away. It was a feeling of painful helplessness, waiting and watching during that time. Cancer is a terrible disease for the patient and for the family as caregivers. The pain of the patient, the pain of the family watching their loved one, is devastating. We depended on the decisions and expertise of many great doctors. Going through this, I at least could talk with doctors for direction and consolation. It was an illness with a name, a diagnosis, and some treatment, but ultimately a sad ending.

After Dad died and Mom seemed like she was able to handle life again, we moved her back to her home, just a mile away. Again we were close by, to help with yard work, doctors, and just wonderful family visits. This type of caregiving and helping out was easier and the way I expected it would be.

After only a couple of months, she went into a depression. I went to visit one evening after work, and she started to cry and say how alone she was with no one to cook for, talk to, or just be needed. Mom and Dad were married for more than fifty years, and now she was alone. She was so accustomed to caring for people, it was not normal for her to be alone. My husband suggested she move in with us, since we had the room. We sold her house, kept the furniture that made part of our home feel like hers, and she lived with us for ten years. Six of those years were wonderful. She had her own living room, bedroom, and bathroom. We shared our kitchen and ate together each evening as a family. With the sale of her home, we helped her establish an investment account, should she need assistance or medical care in her future.

The first few years of Mom's living with us went very well. It was a crazy blend of three generations and a dog. When she moved in after my father died, we spent lots of good times together. Family meals were together, as were weekly shopping, movie nights, and trips with the kids. Mom was a big part of our family. As Mom developed healthy outside friendships and joined the senior center, she was again being her own person and thriving independently, even though in our home. She had her own life with friends again. We had our lives and met in the middle. Three generations under one roof was certainly working. It was great for our children too. A different perspective of the world was shared by Mom. Mom's opinion mattered, and she mattered. She gave extra insight to our children when it came to school, friends, and family. Catherine was a warm and important part of her grandchildren's lives. Those warm memories comfort us now and will always.

Just about the seventh year, slow changes started with Mom, slow enough that we actually let most go, rather than create any tension. The changes were little things that didn't really matter, yet, just gentle aging.

Determining at what point a child should parent a parent was very unsettling. There was an inner battle to do the right thing without overstepping my place or Mom's. She showed signs of a different way of thinking now that we did not fully see until after the fact, at times. When someone has been so independent and rational her entire life, we tend to take that behavior for granted. We did not fully understand what was happening or how complicated it would get.

Personality changes came upon Catherine slowly and subtly before we noticed how serious it was becoming. Many simple situations with Mom became a mystery for me to figure out. We knew our parents as very competent all our lives, so the subtle changes were not always recognizable. Living in the same house, changes in behavior were probably picked up sooner than if a caregiver stopped by to visit occasionally. It appeared that Catherine became more impulsive rather than giving thought to some actions. If this turns out to be true for me as I age, I have warned my children to keep me away from shoe stores!

I found myself entering a world I did not want. I did not want to be a mother to my mother, and I didn't know how to go about it without hurting "us" and the beautiful relationship we shared. One of the reasons we loved and respected Catherine was her great strength and determination. Now that strength and determination became her defense and our nemesis. She was proud, strong, and did not need or want help. It was becoming clear that she did need our help, though.

There were new feelings now between us. Things were changing for Catherine and also for me, because of the changes in her thinking. Her thought process was changing without her knowledge, and my thinking was changing because of it. I watched cautiously and gently as she began to show signs of perhaps senility, dementia, or just aging. What was happening to Catherine did not really have a name. Since we all lived together, it was important for our family and for Catherine to keep the peace and live together in harmony.

When I was growing up, my mom was always there for me and many times for friends of mine in need, when they didn't feel they could go to their own parents. I could share just about anything with my mom, perhaps too much, but she was always understanding and accepting. Her judgment of me was age appropriate, and I tried to judge her the same at this latter time in her life. It was my turn to try to understand Mom, and it wasn't easy.

Parents of teenagers seemed to compare battle stories and things in common when raising teenagers. I knew of no one parenting a parent while I was. I felt alone and desperate for someone to understand and help me.

Maybe the "terrible twos" and "terrible teens" in raising my children helped me prepare for what could be called the "terrible twilight years" of some of our elderly parents. *Elderly* is thought of as old and frail, but I feel in my heart that the elderly deserve to be dignified and respected for a life traveled over mountains of happiness and valleys of despair and sadness. We as a family respected Mom and gave her full independence well into her eighties. Everyone ages differently, and therefore the care needs to be adjusted to the individual. Sometimes this care and help is misunderstood and rejected by the aging parent.

Our parents have conquered what we are still working at: life! Their strength has worked wonders to help them survive life's journey, but it can also work against the caregiver as an elder parent becomes frail or confused. I look back at caring for Mom, and now I am grateful for having that chance. Going through it, however, was trying at times, to say the least. It was one of the hardest things I've had to deal with. The hardest part was the fact it seemed endless those last few years.

For those of you facing this task of unselfishly caring, please don't be too hard on yourself. You really won't see how strong and unselfish you are until well after all is over. Time will help you understand and see things clearer. It was at most times more difficult than raising my children. You can give your children rules and consequences. The end result usually is that the children grow up, mature and understand the path of a responsible adult. The end result with an elder parent dealing with senility or dementia of some sort is not those things, and you can't see a light at the end of the tunnel. There are varying levels of dementia or senility. How can you give consequences to your parent, and what would they be? Stay in your room? You are grounded? Take a time out? Sadly the parent does not improve and you can't make the parent better. As a mother we want to fix things for our children and our families and make everything all better. Some things we can't make better, and we just have to maintain some balance for everyone.

Years later I now look at others helping parents. Some have thought it was more difficult for me without a sibling to help out. Whether you have a sibling or not, both situations come with their own set of problems. I alone had full responsibility in giving care and making the right decisions. Dealing with siblings can work if they all work together and see what the other is dealing with; however, there are many reasons why children and siblings choose to deal with an aging parent or choose not to. Each situation is unique, and looking at it objectively may give you more understanding. I watch others caring for their parent now, and some are dealing with some frustration because of a sibling's lack of help or care or because of a sibling's questionable judgment. We don't know their stories. One sibling could be in denial or one may have a history with his or her parent that either distanced them from the situation or made them able to care for a parent. Each situation is as different as the individuals themselves. There are also those who appear to have things under control, and they reject any suggestions. Each situation is unique, and who are we to criticize, as long as the parent is cared for responsibly and safely? I had no additional pressure or help by a sibling because of the loss of my sibling. All families are different, so it works differently for each. It was me, my decisions, and my devotion. It was also my heartbreak and constant self-questioning to make sure I did the right thing. Along with those things came my regrets or disappointment with myself for not being stronger, more patient, and more understanding, but not more loving. I loved Mom completely, and what a test of love it became!

The simple problems started when Mom would answer our phone for us while we were at work. She had her own phone, so I mentioned it was not necessary to answer ours; let it go to voicemail. Nope, she could handle it. No, she couldn't, but we would not be telling her otherwise. Many a doctor or dentist appointment was canceled for us and messages were misinterpreted. Those things were minor, we thought; easy to fix, not worth any long discussions that might be upsetting. She was old. She said she understood, but it didn't change things. We shook our heads and smiled and sighed as phone messages were confused.

Catherine was a "people person" and was friendly and helpful to everyone, so when strangers or salespeople called, it was a time for her to be friendly. If strangers came to the front door and needed to use our phone, it was a time to be helpful. There she was, alone in our home, telling callers her life story and inviting strangers in to use the phone because they said their car broke down or they were lost. Just by the grace of God, nothing bad happened. We could only hope that after we explained how this behavior could be dangerous, she didn't do this again. We could only hope, because we never found out otherwise. We did have suspicions as to whether she understood. It was much like warning my children about strangers, but I wasn't sure Catherine would listen to us. Whether she did or did not, she knew not to tell us.

Things were going along well, I thought, until she called me at work saying her face was a bit swollen. I asked her to call the doctor and set up an appointment, and I would leave work to take her to her appointment. I left work, and as we were driving to the doctor, she mentioned she should probably tell the doctor about her leg. I didn't know there was a problem with her leg, and then she showed me. There was a wound the circumference of a silver dollar; and it was deep. Ugh! I told her she absolutely had to tell the doctor. I didn't want to join her with the doctor, for fear of making her feel childlike, and she agreed. This was the beginning of three years of the breakdown of not only her health, but also our relationship. The signs were no longer as subtle, and it had become a health issue. I had to watch and listen more carefully for her safety. It took three years of multiple skin grafts, vascular surgery for blood flow, numerous doctor and hospital visits, and me dressing her leg wound twice each day to finally get the awful wound to heal. At her age, one health issue led to another. Because of about sixty years of smoking, her circulation was weak and the wound took forever to heal. Juggling work, family, and mom's health issues became very demanding. Caregiving is exhausting emotionally and physically, but we had only begun. It did not help that Catherine would listen to doctors' orders only sometimes.

Mom's physical issues signified the beginning of years of turmoil both physically and mentally. In addition to her wound and circulation problems, she needed kidney specialists, carotid artery surgery, and more frequent doctor visits. During those years I had to give her constant care to dress the wound, but more frustrating was the fact that Mom would listen to doctor instructions only sometimes, which led to tension between us almost daily while I tried to help her understand. To get better one must do what the doctor orders. The doctors were great, but she thought of the money and not her health. She had her small income and savings, but she did not want to spend it on medical care. Her pension and Social Security income was all hers each month, since she lived with us, and she had an investment of about $40,000, should her health issues become more serious. She also had her health insurance. She lived with us all expenses paid, and one more person certainly was no drain financially for us.

I was fortunate to work for a very compassionate employer who allowed me to leave work early one day a week for doctor visits to check her skin grafts. Making up the time or work was never a problem. Her wound was stubborn and needed constant checking by the physician as well as our care at home. I would get up by 5:00 a.m. each day to dress her wound before getting myself ready for work. As soon as I returned from work I dressed the wound again. I followed the doctor's instructions explicitly. She was told to take short walks a couple times a day to help with blood flow, which would also expedite healing. Mom insisted she was walking, but when my children were home from school we realized she was not moving from her chair. We even had a stationery bike, but it sat and so did she. How do you make someone listen? What do you do when the person insists she is following doctor's orders and you know she is not? There was nothing that would make her listen or understand, and she grew defiant with us. At least two-year-olds or teenagers most often "get it" finally. My parent would not. She was strong and certainly would not be told by her child what to do. As I tried delicately, and I mean delicately, to share with her doctors that I thought she should be more mobile, I watched as Catherine actually lied to the doctors.

This could not be my mother, I thought. I did learn that her doctors were very familiar with elderly patients and had seen this behavior before. Their understanding was a blessing to me. The doctors understood Catherine, and they also understood what we caregivers were going through. My husband's and my vacations were planned around her surgeries and health issues. I don't mean we went on vacation before or after; I mean vacations were spent nursing her back to health. At that time there was no family leave policy. Again, in my heart and soul we did not give it a second thought. We cared and loved her. We just did it. There are many caregivers with unselfish hearts out there. Yes, it is difficult, but the day will come and you will be happy that you cared. I will admit the balancing of career, family, and caring for my mom was draining physically, but more emotionally. To this day, we as a family have no regrets. To this day I wonder how we did it all!

There are many strains on a marriage, and taking care of Mother was only one we faced. In his heart, my husband knew that my parents loved him like a son and were always there for him and our family, which is why my husband was such a great support. They were not well off, so it wasn't financial support; it was simply love, time, and caring for our family. Their wealth was love.

One day I thought it might be a good idea to check on Mom's investments, seeing how health issues were starting to develop. We never knew how or when things could get worse. I asked to see her latest statement and maybe have her check with her financial advisor, not me, to see where it could be best invested or changed, if it even needed to be. My mom's money was hers, not mine. While reading the statement, it didn't look like it changed in the least, so maybe it would be a good idea to inquire. Oops! I noticed the date on the statement. It was a couple of years old. I asked to see a more recent one, and my heart sank as she brought the newer statement. My heart sank not because of the newer statement, but the way my mom looked. For the first time she stood like a child, hands clasped together, looking like she was guilty of something. Dear God, why and what was going on here? Almost $35,000 was gone and only $6,000 was left. What happened to it all? Her response was she had her bills, but she didn't have any bills other than her supplemental health insurance. Her income was just over $1,100 a month, of which we asked for nothing. Her medical expenses were mostly covered by Medicare and her supplemental insurance. She had no living expenses at all. What right did I have to monitor and question her, though? She was the mother and I the child. She lived independently for so long and paid her bills not only on time but ahead of time. Where was the money going? Had she forgotten this small investment was for her if she were to need assisted living or a nursing home?

I asked to see her checkbook. As I looked at the entries, which by the way were calculated perfectly, I saw hundreds of dollars a month going to cash, charities, and a popular contest promising financial wealth. Each and every month hundreds were spent this way. Letters I found years later to those contests were written by Catherine so they would know what a loyal contributor she was and how much she needed to win. It seemed like her desperate attempt to beg them to let her win. I felt sick inside. What right did I have to do anything?

I was spinning and didn't know what to do or say. I tried to help her understand that charity donations were for people who could afford to donate, and that she was not going to win the fortune of a lifetime. Her investment was mostly gone, and I secretly did not want to know anything else. I hated to face more of what was happening, and I hated being a mother to my mother.

I asked that she put the money given to charities and contests into savings. I had hoped that by this discussion—and it was a discussion, not an argument—that she would get it: listen. I didn't want to be her mother. I then set up a savings account for her so she would at least have something should she need it for medicine, incidentals, or even holiday shopping. We were already picking up some of her expenses when she didn't have enough to cover some medications, and now we knew why. We would never say no to medication or anything she really needed. One medicine alone was almost $300 and not covered by her insurance. She could reimburse us if she had it. When we set up a savings account for her, she now saw it as we were taking her money and not saving it for her. Her name was on that account, to be used only by her, but that was not what she heard. This was a step to control something, for a good reason, we thought. It seemed like a logical thing to do to help her, but she did not accept it as that. Mom was furious. Had we been financially secure ourselves, it wouldn't matter. We were blue collar, middle class people putting three children through college. We wanted to help Mom as much as possible, but it was getting out of control in many ways.

As I mentioned earlier about addictive traits in Catherine's family, this is where those ugly traits in Catherine's family became evident.

Gambling was the major ugly trait that seemed to take over. On her grandchild's birthday, she gave a birthday card with $15 in it. The children were always very appreciative of anything given and never felt entitled. My mom apologized that it was all she could afford with her limited income. This was fine if it weren't for the fact she then asked her grandchild to take her to the local store to pick up a couple of things. When they both entered the store, the salespeople greeted her loudly, "Hey gamblin' granny, how are ya?" As my mom dropped $50 for lottery tickets, her grandchild stood in embarrassment. The sales help was laughing at her grandmother. "See you tomorrow, gambling granny," they said.

Grandmother and grandchild returned home, I could see on my child's face that something was wrong. My children did not want to betray their grandmother, but I asked privately what happened. I could only imagine how much money was also going to the lottery. No wonder there were so many checks made out to cash in her checkbook. I did not have the heart or strength to address the issue. I wanted to cry, so I did. Was she out of control? Where do you get help for this problem? How many times a day, a week did it happen? I resolved myself to the fact that it was her money and she was cared for by us, so if she wanted to spend her money that way, so be it. I was still at least saving some of her money in her new account. She had everything else she needed, living with us.

As time went on, I found myself coming home from work, making a cup of tea for myself, and going to my bedroom to unwind, gain more strength to face Mom, and take on my evening tasks with a smile on my face and a knot in my stomach. Our relationship was fracturing. She was spiraling downward and emotionally pulling us with her. I would then start dinner and we would sit together, eat as a family, and have strained small talk. Nothing we said mattered anymore to her. Our frustration and worry only grew. She was always a part of our home, but now we were feeling we were a part of *her* home. By that I mean that it seemed everything in our home was revolving around Mom and whatever was going to happen next.

She continued to face numerous skin grafts, and if she did not have enough money to cover any medicines or bandages, we had her small account or we supplemented her payments, which was another strain for us. We were fighting a losing battle and there was no winner.

Catherine was scheduled for the third and, we hoped, the final skin graft in hopes of it healing. She decided not to allow the same plastic surgeon to perform the surgery because she no longer liked him. With all his patience and expertise, he too was losing some patience and became more firm in his instructions to Catherine, which did not sit well with Catherine. She was not going to listen to him either. She asked her vascular surgeon to perform the skin graft, which I didn't understand how he could, since it was not his field. In the recovery room, however, after that final skin graft, the original plastic surgeon came in to see how she was doing. Catherine immediately asked him what he was doing there, and he mentioned he heard she was in the hospital and wanted to see how she was. He smiled at me, smiled at Catherine, and I formed my own conclusion as to why he was there and felt relieved. He was one of the best.

We were fortunate after the last skin graft surgery to have a visiting nurse come for a couple of weeks to help dress and bandage the wound. It was a welcomed reprieve, especially for me. I would have to dress the wound only once a day, in the evening. The nurse loved my mom, so I hoped it would stay that way. The mother I knew, loved, and trusted was disappearing to us. The nurse's children would send my mom pictures they drew, and my mom would send them candy or treats. I shared nothing of our issues with the visiting nurse. Their relationship was good, and I felt there was no reason to complicate it.

One evening, however, the visiting nurse called me. I could hear the frustration in her voice. "Oh dear, what the heck happened?" I asked, and, not surprised, I heard how she thought my mom was milking this situation. She wasn't listening to her instructions, and she wasn't doing what the nurse asked of her to help herself heal. The nurse was upset that Mom's kindness was not authentic, and the nurse just couldn't deal with it any longer. She actually said what I was thinking and seeing for so long. Without any details I shared with her just a bit of our frustration and what we were facing. I apologized to the nurse, but she did not return. I felt awful, but in some way I felt validated. I then began my old routine of 5:00 a.m. and evening bandage detail.

As the caregiver it became clearer to me that Mom and I were interpreting prescription dosages and doctors' instructions differently, or perhaps Mom was just going to do it her way. As we repeated the instructions to make sure she understood, she would confidently acknowledge the information, and she would actually repeat it. We would discover she really didn't follow the instructions.

I always made sure my mom's medications were promptly filled and reminded her of the times and dosage and left notes for her. She was not incoherent and could really function with daily routines. I checked and counted pills and made sure she was safe. As she did to the visiting nurse, Catherine looked to me to be in control, but I knew now to question and check everything.

Returning from work one day, I found her crawling on the floor looking inside a closet. When I asked what was happening, she said she was looking for prune juice. We had some in the fridge, and I poured her a glass and asked what was going on. At the same time, I noticed feces on various spots on the floor, which was not like her at all. She was meticulous. She looked a bit strange, and as I questioned her, I realized she was very confused. Stroke? Or medicine? I immediately got the medication from her cabinet and realized more were missing than should be. She had always been able to have a conversation and make sense. She was not confused about taking care of herself; she thought she knew better. Her finances? It was her money, and she knew what she was doing and could do what she wanted. Now the medicine! This situation was getting worse.

When she complained about her pain from her surgery she always mentioned that she never liked taking medicine. She said to all her doctors, "I'm not one for medicine." The visiting nurse said the pain medication was prescribed to her and she should take it when she needed to. My mom heard "needed" and not the prescribed every six hours. She also was prescribed medication to thin her blood. She asked one doctor how long she would need to take this medicine. The doctor said until we get your blood thinner and at a good level. Her thought must have been if she took an additional dose, the blood would thin sooner and she wouldn't have to take or pay for the medicine any longer. We realized this possibility one evening when we were shocked to see the blood vessels in her eyes broken, and we immediately called the doctor. She explained what she had done, and from that day on, we left only the medicine needed on a particular day for her. Now I would leave the prescribed dose and hide the medication while I was at work. If I had thought her to be incoherent in any way, I would have done this sooner. No nurse or doctor thought it either. She was sweet and cooperative in the office.

Quickly, after we controlled the medicine for her, she was back to normal - whatever normal was now! Catherine could function. She got up, got washed, brushed her teeth, ate breakfast, got dressed, and went to the senior center most days. Bedtime routine was also normal.

After the three years and the success of the wound healing, she started to join her friends at the senior center more often again, started living again outside with friends. It was good for her and for us. I got a break and foolishly thought things would be fine from then on. Her health was good, finances, oh well, water under the bridge. Life was okay again! Mom seemed happy and we were too.

Mom decided to take a week's vacation with her senior center, and it was such good news, healthy for her to be with peers having fun and healthy for us all. Day one of her vacation, I went to work and came home, checking the mailbox before coming inside. Huh, no mail. We always get some sort of mail, even junk mail. Day two I checked the mailbox before coming inside, and again no mail. Oh, boy. I called my husband at work and said I think Mom stopped the mail before she went away on her trip. My husband said she wouldn't and couldn't. I drove to the post office and asked if there was any mail for my address that was perhaps not delivered. The postman checked in the back and told me there was a Stop Mail order for a week for my address. I proceeded to explain that I owned the home and I would like my mail. The order was placed by my mom and mail would not be delivered until she returned in a week, I was told. Again I tried to explain she was my elderly mother who did this by mistake. He would not budge and said I needed to speak with my mail carrier who would be in at 7:00 the next morning. To say the least, I was upset by the post man, but followed his advice rather than create any more stress. I was not a child asking for my mail, I was fifty years old! My husband was shocked, but by this time my mind was racing with thoughts of "what else?"

I called the post office promptly at 7:00 the next morning. Our mail carrier said that Mom did in fact place a Stop Mail order for her mail while our mail carrier was on vacation, and the covering carrier was confused and stopped all the mail to our home. Usually, I was told, Mom only stopped her own mail to our home when she went away, even if only for a day, which was odd—to our delivery person, but not to me. It was Mom's way of hiding what was delivered to her, like a child catching the mail before the parents got home, so report cards or absence notices might not be discovered. My children didn't even do this! She would bring in the mail each day and leave ours on the table for us. We never saw hers, nor did we feel it necessary. I asked our delivery person to please bring all the mail that day and disregard the stop order. That day she delivered stacks of magazines and notices of great prizes to be won. We realized that nothing was okay; it was just hidden better.

Mom returned from her trip. We waited to address the problem, and the dialogue went like this:

> My husband: Why did you stop the mail to our house?
>
> Mom: I never stopped your mail.
>
> My husband: Are you telling me you never stopped the mail to our house?
>
> Mom: I never stopped your mail.
>
> My husband: Let me ask it differently. Have you ever stopped any mail to this house, yours or ours, at any time?
>
> Mom: Um, I can't quite recall.

I couldn't take much more. I made an appointment with our family doctor for help, advice, anything. I was sobbing as I told my story. He was understanding as I explained what was happening with Mom. I asked if I could get help for her. She was definitely having trouble with finances, gambling, and interpreting things. I explained that as we supervised her more, she didn't seem to be a danger to herself or others. He said she was really a financial danger to herself and obviously now needed adult supervision; however, he said if she wasn't willing and didn't recognize she had a problem, it would not help her. He could recommend a counselor for me if we were having trouble dealing with the situation. My mom would not ever admit to having any problem, and quite honestly I believed she didn't see there was a problem other than with our intervention. We tried to give her some constructive criticism, and then we continued to hope that she would get it, get something!

As she went on with her senior friends, we went on with our lives again. We wondered when, not if, the next shoe would drop. She did start separating herself from us by closing the door to her part of the house. Our relationship was more than fractured; it was broken. We tried to remain civil and keep the peace. There was such a sadness in our home at that time. My stress was relieved by verbalizing it with my husband who just didn't want to listen anymore and my dearest friends, Jean and Penelope, and I don't understand how they listened to me so much. My sanity came from the compassion of my family and friends. My patience and understanding were deteriorating quickly. In hindsight, I should have sought that counselor my doctor suggested. We lived under the same roof, but a sad roof.

Everyone moved on, or so we thought. I didn't think things could get worse, but was shocked to find out again they could, and did. One evening I went to the grocery store and my husband received a phone call from my mom's lawyer, who was also our lawyer. He knew our family well by this time, and being an elder attorney, understood what was happening. When my mom first sold her house, she purchased a small cabin in the southern Adirondacks, in addition to establishing an investment for herself. The cabin was something she and my dad wanted and something for our whole family. Since she was moving in with us, there would be no expenses for her, a portion invested in the cabin, and more than $40,000 investment for her when needed for future medical care. Mom would use the cabin with friends and she would join us. We agreed to maintain the expenses, since she had made the initial investment. We would take her with us for weekends and vacations. Our children often used it, and we invested our time and money into improving it for all of us to enjoy. As years passed, she added my name to the deed, and then eventually decided to add her grandchildren's names to the deed. We were carrying all expenses and she was settled, at least at that time. All of this was done through an attorney and many years before the slightest sign of any problem.

On the evening our lawyer called, he was beside himself with anger. Apparently my mom made a visit to his office, and since he was busy at that moment, she met with his new associate. Mom told a story of how I was going to help her change the deed to the cabin to include our children's names, along with hers and mine. The deed she presented did not show her grandchildren's names. She wanted my children on the deed along with her name and mine. The new associate attorney was going to save the day for what she thought was a senior citizen taken advantage of. Mom had forgotten the issue was taken care of years before. The attorney apparently jumped to the conclusion that it could be a case for Social Services and shared this conclusion with Mom, assuming the change was done without Catherine's consent.

When she asked my mom who the attorney was, my mom said the name of the attorney's partner. With that I can only imagine the attorney's thought, and she then excused herself, quickly, to consult with her associate, our attorney. Welcome to the world of Mom's gray maze and those trying to keep her safe in so many aspects. Catherine's world was expanding and causing more problems, without her realizing how much damage she was doing to others. What actually happened was my mom had an old copy of the deed, and upon seeing the new deed, realized it was exactly how she had instructed almost fifteen years earlier. No one was undermining her.

Our attorney was upset, and rightfully so, because if she had gone to a different attorney, it could most definitely have been misinterpreted and he could have been falsely accused. This was the last straw, but of course it caused more upset and much more guilt.

I was falling apart, my family was strained and arguing, my husband and I were cracking, but my mother didn't get this, and neither did it seem to matter to her. The strangest thing was that Catherine really did not see the extent of her actions.

The next day, however, I received a phone call from that new "save-the-day" associate lawyer apologizing for the misunderstanding. Apparently Catherine had called her to explain and apologize for this misunderstanding. I asked the attorney if she believed every elderly person who walked through her door and was so quick to accuse the people who completely cared for their parents in every way humanly possible. How dare she jump on the abuse wagon when we were the ones feeling abused and helpless?

My mother took care of all her legal issues well before she became loopy, meeting privately with attorneys and never being coerced in any way. Why? Why? Everything was done the right and legal way with a good attorney because we are good people and wanted to cover all our bases legally. I'm thinking this attorney also learned a good lesson that day. The attorney was extremely upset with herself, as was I. I had looked after my parents since I was seventeen years old. I was never looking for financial gain. I had seen doctors and lawyers to make sure I did it right. What more could someone do? In hindsight again, if the cabin was not purchased and protected in some way, all those finances probably would have gone to charities and mail-in contests.

My house was sad and silent for a long time, again. We talked about the weather, our jobs, and school. We were at the end of our rope. I loved Mother, but did not like what she was doing or turning into through no fault of her own. Things were out of control, and it wasn't affecting only our immediate family but others outside now. A doctor said it was not Alzheimer's, because patients do not think in the depth she did, almost calculating. She could have a level of dementia.

Our home was shattered. Our family of five was spinning and my mom was oblivious to the circumstances. I really don't think Catherine understood how serious things were becoming.

Catherine had enough also. She decided she would move into a semi-assisted senior apartment complex where many of her friends lived. She explained she was not a child and wanted to move near her friends. Being that she was a strong and determined person, there was no stopping her as much as there was no making her understand what was happening.

Her rent and expenses in her apartment would be based on her income, and we would be here to supplement anything she might need as we always were. We were there to pick up the pieces. Full meals, soup to nuts, were served daily, and the place was beautifully maintained. There was an on-site person should there be any issues, and that person knew to call us for anything. We were then on top of things without her ever knowing it. It was good for her and for us. We all had much healing to do; however, I was destroyed, guilt ridden, angry, hurt, frustrated, and depressed for what happened to our relationship, my family, and to my mom. I felt I failed her, even after ten years of caring for her. My whole family was still there for her, but just behind the scenes. Our visits were much nicer now. She felt independent and was, for the most part. There were constant checks and balances, but by each of us, and it worked better for each of us.

For those of you in the middle of this situation, my heart goes out to each and every one of you. Whether your parent is living with you or you are the number-one caregiver on call 24/7, you have my utmost respect and compassion. As I said before, we can't help our feelings, but we can help how we act or react. Should I have just not taken it so hard? She was old; that's what everyone would say. Not taking it hard is much easier said than done when you are in the thick of things. The strain lessened with Mom living in a senior complex. It was close to our home and we visited often. She came for dinner, and we still managed time together. We both were different people, as a result. We healed a bit, I guess, but I will always wonder if she ever understood any of what happened. I, myself, have learned so much, again from my mom.

Catherine, once living alone, depended more on our oldest son and daughter-in-law. If questions arose or there were any concerns, the staff would confer with us, which was critical now that she was again on her own. Honest, open communication within our family for Catherine's well-being was of the utmost importance. Again, there was sadness in my heart that our older son and his wife were thrown into this new, strange responsibility. It didn't seem fair. Our two younger children kept in closer contact with Catherine too. I was proud of my children of how they instinctively knew to be there for their grandmother and our family. Nana taught us all well.

Unless you have parented a parent under the same roof, it may be difficult to fully understand the new dynamics. Many say they understand, and there are many more with lots of advice, but unless you live it, you don't really get it. For those of you caring for parents outside of your homes, it is hard enough. This setup too comes with its own set of problems, and you wonder if they are really fine. When you visit you wonder if all is what it appears to be. When we were living under one roof, the state of the situation was easier to detect but not easier to accept. My mom became the teenager who doesn't listen, who is rebellious, and who is calculating, but you always love with all your heart and want her to get it. God willing, teenagers do eventually get it, but it's usually a one-way ticket with an elderly parent, one you trusted, loved, and looked up to. One who took care of you.

My dearest friends who sadly lost their parents far too young may not have experienced my issues but had their own sadness because of the loss of their parents far too prematurely. Their sadness came far too early. Their families missed many good times, before the gray clouds moved in. My heart feels for them and the void in their lives.

Things seemed to be going well for Mom and all of us again, or so we thought. She was settled in her new home; our home was settling for us again. We thought things were back to a normal.

It wasn't over! I received a call from my mom's doctor one evening. He was the most caring and understanding doctor to our situation and his patients' health and safety came first. My mom had left his office with her friend and was headed to our local hospital with symptoms of a possibly mild heart attack. She refused an ambulance but assured him they were on their way to the ER. He wanted us to know the situation just in case it too became confusing.

It took my family and me three hours to track Mom down. Yes, she went to the hospital she was directed to, but she and her friend decided to shop at the dollar store first and then go out for Chinese food, because one never knew how long a wait it would be in the emergency room. She eventually had a heart-valve replacement from which she recuperated perfectly. She then came home and was doing very well until she got pneumonia the following winter and simply couldn't come back after it. My heart still cries for her, for our damaged relationship, our family's relationship, and for the feelings that I wish I could have changed. If only I could do it all again with the clearer understanding that I have now, an understanding that comes with time and hearing stories of others facing the same challenge and all the feelings wrapped up in it. I felt guilty for not being better at handling the situation.

We share this story for our children who, we hope, have learned from us as we have learned from our parents. I was not fully prepared for this journey. I know my children have seen the happiness and sadness in all of this. I hope it helps them be better caregivers when their turn comes. This is the way of life. Life, to me, is about family first. It seems we love, protect, and raise our children and then they love, protect, and raise us.

My children, my husband, and dear friends Jean and Penelope continued to help me cope with my emotions and helped me understand that my mom was the one changing, and I simply couldn't change with her. I had to be the parent of my parent. My children gently would say, "Nana just isn't Nana anymore." I tried hard to keep reminding myself of that fact. Catherine's changes were not intentional, and one can try hard not to take it personally, but at times we can't help it. We try to understand that our parents can no longer help their feelings either. Did I do this perfectly? Absolutely not! I am human, and I say this to all of you who will face the roller coaster of emotions that arise when caring for a loved one. You are human, and being human, we have weaknesses and are not perfect, and that's because we are human! We may have a difficult time controlling our feelings, but we can control how we act and react. I would have been truly lost without my family and friends to hold me up.

Years after, when I began to understand what had happened and tried to deal with my emotions, which were by then settling, I met my friend Ann at work. You just know when a friendship clicks! The older we get, the more careful I think we are about good friends. I have been blessed by many for years. I love them like family and run to them for moral support. Ann's and my story also clicked and helped heal us both.

My healing took years. I was hurt and guilt ridden. How did everything get so confusing? It took so much time to understand what actually happened and time to forgive myself for feeling the hurt, the anger, and mistrust.

As years went by, some people who knew what I went through came to me to vent with their own similar stories, to perhaps hope for understanding as they dealt with caring for an elderly parent. I heard clearly and understood well what they were going through. My heart hurts for them. I only hope I helped them, consoled them, and helped them look and see more clearly than I once did inside that gray, wrinkled, cloudy world.

CHAPTER 6

Navigating In The Fog

The aging process can present itself in many different ways and so slowly and subtly that it can almost go unnoticed. Martha's entrance into that world had, unbeknown to me, already begun when she came to live with me; however, unlike Catherine, my mom began to step back and assume she was a burden and not worthy of love. I'm not sure it was necessarily a conscious decision, but just a continuation of how she may have perceived herself for many years.

Mom's self-worth came from how hard she worked, how busy she kept, and how much she was needed. When she came to live with me, I believe somehow she stepped back in time and felt it was her job to take care of me again. As she became less able to be busy all the time and she discovered that not only was I capable of taking care of myself, but that I also preferred it, her self-worth faded. Cooking was her way of showing love and feeling valuable. Even when she and my stepdad were in their eighties, they were the first to show up on a sick friend's doorstep with a pot of soup. Being there to listen to all of us when we were struggling with life's challenges fed her soul. How do you tell your mom that she has become your biggest life challenge?

One March evening, mom suffered what we believe was a mini-stroke. I got the call at 7:00 p. m. that night and made the three-hour trip to the hospital in record time. When I arrived, she was sitting up smiling, looking like she always did. We took her home that night with no more than a new prescription for blood-pressure medication. Phew, thank goodness she suffered no permanent damage.

Within a week she began hallucinating and became hysterical. She was sure things were pushing up through the basement floor, that there was mud running down the walls, and that someone was playing the organ in the background all the time. One night at 3:00 a. m., I received a call from my stepdad saying she was screaming that someone was taking her baby. I'm not sure if she was referring to me or my brother. I got on the phone with her and assured her we were okay. She calmed down somewhat, and my stepdad said he was going to call an ambulance. They were both eighty-seven and he was worn down. I jumped into the car and made the trip, once again in record time, to see what needed to be done.

When I arrived at the hospital, she was still terribly confused. The doctors wanted to send her home. They told me that be-cause I lived out of town, I probably didn't notice how much she was slipping, and that this was just an advancement of her dementia. My mom may have been slowing down, but one does not go from totally taking care of herself and her husband, spending hours chatting logically and coherently with me on the weekends when I visited, overnight to hallucinating and total desperation.

I convinced the doctor to admit her for observation and testing to see if something was going on to cause her sudden change in behavior. When she went to the hospital, her medicine list didn't go with her. The staff asked me what medications she was taking, and I told them what I knew off the top of my head, forgetting the new blood-pressure medication she had been put on. Each day she was hospitalized we noticed a decrease in her hallucinations. She became more aware of who people were. She seemed to be improving; however, she was nowhere near ready to go home. The doctor said she would have to enter a dementia ward in a nursing home. On the third day I discovered the nurses weren't giving her the blood pressure medication, thus the decrease in hallucinations. It was a medication side-effect, and if we hadn't picked up on it, the doctors never would have, and she would have been placed somewhere that was totally inappropriate.

After the incident, which was something that just about did us all in, things settled down and she was, for the most part, her typical self; however, it really shattered her sense of well-being. She was terrified of losing control of her thoughts and needed constant reassurance that she was doing fine and that the confusion was a direct result of the change in medication.

My concerns then turned to my stepdad. Mom's event took a serious toll on him. He was always large and in charge in a good way, and he didn't know how, nor did he have the energy, to take care of things during this time with Mom. He turned it over to my brother and me, something that was very out of character for him and something that took away his own self-worth, which revolved around being able to take care of his wife.

I relate all this information because it will be helpful to see how this new lack of self-confidence affected my mom's gradual decline and the way she responded to the events that unfolded. It is probably important for me to mention where I was in my own life at the time all this started to unfold. I had just begun to recover from the breakup of a thirty-two-year marriage; I had moved to a new apartment and was working full-time, enjoying my three-year-old grandson, and excited about the birth of a second. I spent most of my weekends alternating between trips to my parents', my daughters, or taking care of my oldest daughter, who had a disability and lived in a group home nearby. I had lots on my plate, but I was managing; in fact, I was thriving and my confidence was soaring. I had lost weight, started going to the gym, and was on a spiritual high. Unlike my mom, my self-value at that time came not from how much I was needed or what I could do for everyone, but merely from my "being." And then everything came to a screeching halt and I was going to have to start all over again with a new life experience.

Six months after my mom's encounter with the medication reaction, my stepdad had a massive heart attack. Somehow he miraculously was sitting up in bed the next morning like nothing ever happened. Our excitement over his survival was short lived. He developed pneumonia and passed away shortly thereafter. And that is when everything turned upside down.

Two days before mother's husband died, she told me the two of them decided that it would be best if she moved in with me. We had talked about what she would do if something happened to him first, but I had always been cautious about inviting her to live *with* me. I had always said *near* me. I could count on one hand how many times my mother had said no when I needed help. I was not about to tell her no at such a vulnerable time in her life.

Mom and I were always very close; however, her announcement blew me right out of the water. Mom didn't want to stay in her home. My apartment was too small for both of us. If she came to live with me she would be alone all day while I was at work. I had retirement plans to move near my daughter and her family, but that move was still a couple years away. To go now could seriously affect my financial security, and yet here we were. Mom had made her decision.

My daughter and son-in-law were very concerned. They knew that staying where I was would not necessarily be the best thing for anyone. I would be very isolated with no family nearby to help. The house next door to them was for sale, and they encouraged me to consider buying it. That way mom would be with me and be able to watch her great-grandchildren grow, and I would have the support from my children. After sorting through all the pros and cons and with Mom's blessing, I decided that plan would be the best for all of us.

I bought the house, started the process for relocating my daughter from one group home to another, put in my retirement papers, and started the huge undertaking of moving three households to another city.

Since I agreed to take on the bulk of Mom's care, my brother and sister-in-law said Mom could spend the winter months with them in the South, escape some of our harsh winter, and give me a break. We thought Mom agreed. She listened and nodded her head, but she hadn't agreed. Over the next five years, she went with them only a handful of times and only for a week or so, and she always wanted me to go with her.

And so the real story begins. It is difficult for me to write this book, because unlike Louise, my mom has been gone only a short time. It is still hard for me to sort through the emotions and events because my emotions are still raw. Perhaps this is a good thing. Grieving is a process. It's a long process. This book gives the opportunity for you, the reader, to see the process and believe that it does get better. I would like to say I was a logical and together person during the time Mom was with me, but I wasn't; I was a crazy lady. I was angry most of the time, impatient, although I tried not to let it show, and guilty that I couldn't embrace the last opportunity to spend time with Mom.

The first sign I had that something was different with Mom was her reaction to the move. She couldn't get out of her house fast enough and was very angry that it took three months for me to arrange the move. I tried to ease the time by having her stay with me in my apartment, but she didn't want that. She seemed to have no concept of the enormity of the situation and thought I was lying to her and dragging my feet. She had been retired so long that I gave her the benefit of the doubt and thought she couldn't relate to being my age any longer and the many responsibilities I had. I traveled every weekend either to her house to help her pack, to our new city to look for group homes for my daughter, and arrange for inspections and all that goes along with buying a house. I was not dragging my feet.

When I did go to her on weekends, I was stunned at all the things she was bringing with her. I had a full house that I was moving with me. Mom had never been a material person. Things meant nothing to her. There was a time when she married my stepdad that she actually turned her house over to her grandson to live in until she decided to sell it. She left everything there except her clothes. But something was definitely different with her thinking now. She was bringing things that didn't make sense. Perhaps she was trying to hold on to my stepdad, but mostly I think she was afraid we wouldn't have enough. She loved me and trusted me, but I was a woman. She didn't feel safe without a man. In addition to everything she was bringing, she was packing things without wrapping them in packing materials. She was livid with me when I told her that we needed to wrap all the glass or it would be in shards after a long trip in a truck. Her greatest fear of not understanding things was coming true, and she knew it. She truly couldn't comprehend what was required for a move like we were facing.

I kept telling myself that she was grieving and lonely, and once we got settled she would start getting back to her typical self. That wasn't going to happen. Something had happened when she had her mini-stroke, not a sudden plunge into dementia, but her personality was different, her logic was not so logical, and her obsession was increasing.

One thing that I think is important to mention here is my mom had never lived alone and hated ever being alone. She wouldn't live alone, read the paper alone, watch TV alone, cook alone, or go anywhere alone. To her, being alone was probably the worst thing she could imagine. I think this personality trait escalated after her mini-stroke. I remember her being angry if my stepdad spent time on the computer or watched a ballgame. She would complain about being bored. She always taught me that happiness is wanting what you get, not getting what you want. She was no longer able to create her own happiness or accept where we were in life. She was looking for others to fill that void.

I had just spent five years living alone and found that I was comfortable being single. I learned to love solitude, and my home was my refuge. I had a significant spiritual awakening and found comfort and company in my God and never, ever felt alone. The initial seed for this lifelong conversion was planted by my mom, and yet when she needed it most, she didn't seem able to find comfort from it.

This difference almost put me over the edge. I think Mom was expecting more of a spousal relationship than a roommate relationship. Her most recent spousal experience happened when they were both retired. They got up at the same time and sat for an hour reading the paper over breakfast and doing the puzzles. They planned their entire day around each other. Meals were a huge deal. The first words out of my mom's mouth every morning were, "What shall we plan for dinner?"

I, on the other hand, had more things on my list of things to do than my mom could ever have realized. I was so overwhelmed each morning when I woke up that I wanted to pull the covers over my head and go back to sleep. I wasn't used to giving an account of everything I was thinking and planning on doing, and the lack of privacy and expectation of accountability was not what I signed on for. That lack of privacy was perhaps the single biggest issue to adapt to. I'm not sure I ever did adapt. Her world was shrinking, and I was her only lifeline.

When we finally got settled, it had been almost a full year since the initial mini-stroke. I had been running nonstop all over the state for a year, and I was exhausted. Mom hit the ground running and became the parent who was in charge of things and decided what needed to be done and when. The house needed some additional projects done and there was still a lot of paperwork that needed to be done with her finances, but we had made sure the bulk of everything was done. Once we were in, I just needed to be done for a while. Nothing had to be tackled immediately. I thought I would chip away. I didn't plan to address many of the things for a year or two or ever. First of all, my finances were seriously affected by retiring earlier than I should. I needed to find a job, assess where we stood financially, and most of all, rest. I desperately needed rest and solitude. Neither was going to happen for a very long time.

There were warning signs everywhere. Like I mentioned, though, when you are in the middle you can't see clearly. One of the biggest disappointments to me about the move was that I was unable to find a group home for my daughter. Mom was always very close to her grandchildren. They loved her and always enjoyed being with her; however, Sarah was her angel. She worried all the time about her and babied her. Mom was the only one who would ever care for Sarah and keep her for a week so I could have a break. The warning sign was huge; she never thought twice about it when I left Sarah behind. Sarah always came first, but now Mom did. Not only did Mom not worry about Sarah, which by the way we didn't need to, because she is well taken care of and happy, but it never occurred to Mom that it was hard on me. Now my family was still spread out and my most vulnerable child was not with me.

We hear a lot about parenting your parents and role reversal when it applies to taking care of your parents. Believe me when I say you never parent your parents. There may be a role reversal, but you are the only one who notices it, has to act upon it, and somehow ensure both parties come out of it whole.

Everything was urgent to Mom. She saw idleness as unacceptable, especially if there were dishes in the sink. To me, dishes in the sink would be there in the morning when I had more energy. Not only did she want me to do all the things that were my things to do, but she also wanted me to do all the things that bothered her, as well. I spent years trying to overcome the need to have my house perfect. The things that she obsessed over were minute to me, compared to all the other things on my plate, but her world was so small, she couldn't see past those little things. Our way of approaching life was totally different, and we both felt we had moved in with a stranger.

I truly spent the first year or two doing everything I could to make Mom happy. If she thought trees should come down, I would arrange it. If she thought I should plant 700 ivy plants in the yard, I would plant 700 plants. When she got up each morning and decided she was hungry for a specific food, I ran to the store. I played Scrabble with her, tried to find the news station that she liked, and watched the TV shows she wanted. I drew the line with cleaning the basement. She hated that there were boxes in the basement. I then made a connection. She used to hound my stepdad about cleaning the basement after her mini-stroke. During the hallucinations, her biggest issue was that things were pushing up through the basement floor. This obsession had started before she came with me. My stepdad had been living with it, but his loyalty to her would never permit him to say anything to us.

No matter what I did or how hard I tried to please her, nothing was ever enough. She needed a spouse. I was her daughter. Not only couldn't I fulfill what a peer would, I didn't want to.

I finally convinced her to try going to the senior center. She loved to play cards, and I hated cards more than anything. She went one day, and I went to pick her up at the agreed upon time. When I got there, she told me she wasn't ready to go home; she was having too much fun. One of the women asked where we lived and offered to bring Mom home. Thank heavens, she found something she liked to do out of the house. I would possibly get an hour or two alone in the house for the first time in two years. She might make some friends. She went again the next week. The same woman brought her home, and Mom announced she wasn't going back because she didn't think the people liked her there. They apparently played a little different version of pinochle than she was accustomed to, and she didn't have the confidence and self-worth to believe people would be patient with her while she learned; perhaps because she herself was no longer patient. She always wanted to fix things immediately; she could never wait to see if things worked themselves out, and neither could she just let things go.

One day at work I got the call that Mom had fallen, was in the driveway, and couldn't move. I arrived as the ambulance did, and it was pretty obvious she had broken her hip. By then we were two years into this living together thing, and I was exhausted. I was terrified when she fell. Terrified she would die and yes, afraid she wouldn't. I'm not proud to admit that, but I was worried about what she would be capable of if she did recover and wondered if I could continue caregiving for even one more day. She underwent surgery, went to rehab for two weeks, and was angry with me that I didn't spend all my spare time with her there. She wouldn't leave her room or try to meet any of the other women. As always she wanted me, only me. Mom made a full recovery and was home in two weeks.

Mom needed to be needed, but being the only person she needed and depended on was suffocating. Even when others offered to help or visit, she wanted me there. Often my brother or one of her stepchildren would call her on the phone. She would talk for a couple minutes and immediately ask if they wanted to talk to me. She wouldn't make a doctor appointment for herself or even talk to the doctor once she got there. I had to tell him how she felt.

After she broke her hip, she felt even more vulnerable. Even from the beginning she rarely went anywhere with me. Now she was even more hesitant. My brother bought her a transport chair. It was lightweight, so I could easily get it in and out of the car. With the chair she could go with me when we went to the store. She went once or twice, and she decided it was a burden to me. I tried to explain that I enjoyed it when she went with me and that it was, in fact, easier for me. If she was with me, I wasn't worried about her being alone and lonely at home. She solved that problem by agreeing to go with me from then on, but the caveat being that she waited in the car, so instead of leaving her at home in a comfortable setting, I was racing through the store because she was waiting in a running car in the parking lot. I have to admit that I can now chuckle about that. At the time it was happening though, it was exasperating.

One summer my children asked me to go to Disney World with them. I just wasn't going to miss that chance. My brother said Mom could stay with him and his wife. I flew with her to his house and stayed a few days, and then I flew on to Disney World for four days. When I left, Mom was coughing. I checked with my brother each day by text to see how she was. She was quiet and still had the cough, but she said she was okay. When I got back from Florida, she wasn't all right. She had pneumonia, but she never spoke up and told my brother how bad she really felt; she waited for me to get back. We ended up having to stay at my brother's an additional week while she recovered. She waited for me even when she was sick. Me, always me.

My brother told me when Mom came to live with me that if I needed to vent, to feel free to do so, so I did. I e-mailed often. I know most of these things sound trivial, but when you are faced with them day after day after long day, they aren't trivial.

When company would come to visit, Mom would be in what I called "company mode." She would perk up. She forced herself to be pleasant and talkative. She stayed up a little later at night, ate anything they put in front of her, and was willing to go wherever they wanted to take her. If I was at work or went away for a few days, when I returned the visitors would say, "She was fine for us. She ate all kinds of different things and loved them. She went places with us and was talkative and full of life." What I heard was, "It must be you." When they left, she stopped eating, wouldn't go anyplace with me, and went back to her old ways. I know that she felt she could be herself with me and that she felt she had to be the hostess if she had company, but it kept even family from truly seeing what our life was like.

However, one time my brother came to visit. Because he was here, I made plans to go out with a friend for dinner and a movie. Mom never wanted me out much past 7:00 or 8:00, so this was my big chance. I told her I would be late and not to wait up. She needn't worry since someone was here with her. At 9:30 my brother texted me to let me know I would not be coming home to a sleeping house. She would not go to bed until I got home. That was a light bulb moment for him. At last he got it. I also wondered how he must have felt when she would not let him step in. He was fully capable and willing, but she had tunnel vision.

There were many little things that started happening. She went to bed at 7:30 every evening and rarely got up before 9:30 in the morning. She complained about her back pain and how stiff she was. She had back exercises that worked well for her, and I would suggest she do those before she got out of bed so she wouldn't be so stiff when she put her feet on the floor. She would nod her head and say she would try them. The next day it would be the same conversation.

She had a terrible problem with digestion. The doctor prescribed something for GERD, gastroesophageal reflux disease. After she had been on the medicine for a couple weeks, I asked her how she felt, and she said she had stopped taking it a week before, because it didn't do any good. I tried to explain that she needed to give it time. She didn't.

She did have significant problems swallowing, for which there was no solution. We always told her the truth about her test results, but we got to the point where we had to avoid some of the facts. She would get so obsessed that every little twinge would be seen as an escalation of whatever the current diagnosis was. She eventually decided that all her problems were a result of a deviated septum that she was diagnosed with years before. We left it at that. Trying to convince her otherwise was impossible.

Her ability to communicate became increasingly difficult. We noticed that she would withdraw when we were together and not contribute to the conversation. When she talked with friends on the phone she would hang up and say they had nothing to say. She had impaired hearing, so I could always hear the other end of the conversation. Mom was the one who had nothing to say. She had always thrived on drama, and if people were happy, she wasn't interested. She couldn't help if people were happy. One time she was talking to her best friend who lived across the country. Mom had just been placed on oxygen. They talked for a long time. When she hung up I asked her why she didn't tell her friend about the oxygen, and she said, "Oh, I forgot."

Mom had stopped going to church when she moved in with me. I can understand, in a way. She knew everyone in her church in her hometown, and it's hard to start over. I asked if she wanted communion brought to her weekly, and she perked right up. I told her I would call the church to see if someone could come. My purpose was twofold, spiritual enrichment and someone to visit with other than me. Well, Mom thought I was going to be the minister, but she hesitantly agreed. I would purposely try to stay out of the way when Joan came. Otherwise, Mom wouldn't make the effort to engage. I would hover in another room, and Mom made no effort to get to know the lovely woman.

Mom became overly obsessive and paranoid as time went on. She was sure that people knew that two women lived alone in my house and that we would be raped in our sleep. When I went to Albany to see Sarah, my younger daughter would come over and stay with Mom at night. Even after her family grew to four little boys, two of whom were twins, my mom didn't give her a reprieve. Mom even had an alert button to push if she needed help in the night, but it didn't help. She was afraid of everything.

She refused to open the window in her room, in spite of safety locks on the windows, because we had raccoons nearby, and they might get in.

She was still determined that I was going to self-destruct because I preferred single life to remarrying, and I think she felt a tremendous responsibility to take care of me. I think, too, that she thought my son-in-law and daughter should have been "taking care of me." I'm not sure what that setup looked like in her mind, but I didn't and don't want to be taken care of. I love being independent and being "God reliant" as opposed to people reliant. Someday maybe I'll need assistance, but for now I'm able to care for myself.

Money became a huge obsession with her. I would hear her constantly rummaging around in her room looking at all her statements. One day she decided that we needed to go to the bank to get a safe deposit box for her bonds. I asked her why she was suddenly concerned about them. She said she was worried there would be a fire. I reminded her that everything was in a fireproof box. That was not okay. There could be a fire in the house and the box could fall through the floor, break open, and the bonds would burn. Really?

Mom was not a wealthy woman. She did have enough to ensure a choice in a good nursing home, though, and I worked hard to make sure the money was invested and growing and kept secure in case she needed it. There came a time when she started looking at me with anger and suspicion. Her health had begun to change, and she mentioned a nursing home. I told her that as long as I could manager her care at home, she need not worry about a nursing home. With her next words, I knew the mom I knew was gone. She said, "Well, of course you would say that; all my money is gone." I asked what she meant, and she announced that her one account was down to a few thousand dollars. I hadn't looked at her statements in a while and ran to find one. If the money was gone, she was a victim of identity fraud. I found her statement, and everything was fine. There was no money missing. I showed her the statement. I'm not sure she believed me, even with the financial information written in black and white.

On June 1, the anniversary of my stepdad's birthday, Mom got up and said she felt really weak. She could barely make it from her bed to the couch. She spent the day lying on the couch, something she never, ever did. She never even took a nap, so I knew something was seriously wrong. I suggested we go to the hospital, since it was a Sunday, but she said no. The following day she hadn't improved, so she agreed to go to the doctor and asked for her transport chair. The tests at the doctor's office showed a significant decrease in her oxygen level, and the staff made arrangements for in-home oxygen and said to return in a week.

The oxygen did help her feel less tired, and we returned to the doctor in a week. His advice was to continue on the oxygen but didn't offer an explanation for the sudden change. The next day I called him, and he said her heart valves were failing. He didn't offer any heroics, she had made it clear to him long before that she was ready to leave this world. He indicated that it could be anywhere from six weeks to a year before the end.

I was honest with Mom. It was a surreal discussion. No tears, not emotion, just facts.

That weekend she had another mini-stroke, and I called family to fill them in on the events. For the next four weeks, family members were in and out to say good-bye. Mom started to fail quickly, and we called in hospice.

There were some wonderful, humorous times in the next couple weeks. One night she announced, "This is it."

My daughter asked if she should bring her boys over, and we decided she should. Everyone piled on the bed and Mom held court. I sat in a chair by her bed. I felt strangely removed from the entire experience. I was numb. I couldn't interact, I just watched.

Somehow mom would live another couple weeks. The house was full of family, and I was present physically, but emotionally removed. In all that time I never had that end-of-life chat you always imagine you will have before your mom leaves you. I hope I had said what she needed to hear through the years she was here. I'm not sure she would have understood at that point at any rate. However, one day, Millie, a family member came in, climbed up on the bed with mom, and told her it was okay to go, that her parents were waiting for her, and Jesus was ready to take her home, and when she saw Him, she should run into His arms and He would say, "Thank you, Martha." Millie was our angel that day. She said what I couldn't, and for that I am eternally grateful.

Even with that guidance, she held on. I know in my heart of hearts that she couldn't leave me. She was still worried about my being alone. My brother was married, so he was fine, but me? I finally went in and hugged her. I told her that it was okay to go, that I would be okay, because my brother said he would stay as long as I needed him. I hadn't left the house in two weeks. The next day I told the aide I was going to run quickly to the store and would be back in twenty minutes. Mom left us while I was gone. She died in my daughter's arms. Even in the end she was protecting me and, I believe, passing on my care to my daughter.

I didn't cry; I didn't feel; I was totally void of any feeling at all. I watched everyone around me grieving, and I felt nothing. I wasn't done. I still had responsibilities, and I was afraid if I let it go, it would be months before I would surface again.

I spent six long years watching my mom's end-of-life journey. She slipped away from us a little each day. In her mind she didn't recognize her value. We did. It was never about what she did for us; it was that she was.

I'm not sure I have been able to demonstrate how difficult things were during those six years, how terribly out of control I felt. Certainly I look back and wonder why some of these things were such a big deal, but I spent six years of my life feeling inadequate, angry, impatient, and guilty. Things weren't clear during that time. I was in survival mode. The mom that moved in with me was not the mom I knew. She wanted to be a mom again, and I wanted her to live her life and I wanted to live mine, together but separately, to some degree. It was not to be. She found her self-worth in being needed and doing. I found mine in just being, and I fell back into the "old" me whom I didn't like. She felt she knew what was best for me based on what was best for her.

Parents probably know their children better than anyone ever will. Mom and I had the same core values. My life experiences led me in a different direction than Mom's. Neither was wrong, just different.

It must be difficult to go from being the mom to being dependent on a child. I know it is difficult to go from being the daughter who was always admired and approved of, to being the daughter who didn't measure up.

Mom would often ask me through the years if we made a mistake when we moved in together. I would always say, "It was the only choice," and it was. It was the only choice because when the time came to make the move, everything was so well orchestrated that there was no doubt that there was someone far beyond my abilities organizing everything. It was meant to be. There was no other choice. It was difficult. She missed her brother terribly and we both missed our friends. If I had it to do again, I would still do it. The only other solution would have been to tell her no. I couldn't do that. It would hurt her too much, and to do that would be the same as hurting myself. I would rather have been miserable than hating myself for saying no.

It's been almost two years now since Mom died. I can tell you that I literally slept twelve hours a day for the next January and February. I just withdrew. I wasn't depressed. I was giving in to my exhaustion and to my grief. I needed time for God to heal me, and I couldn't do it without isolating myself.

I'm beginning to feel again. I'm beginning to remember good times again. I'm beginning to miss her, finally. It takes time. It is an all-consuming experience, and the emotions are so tangled that processing them is tumultuous.

Of this I am sure: my value comes from "being." It does not come from how much I do, how much I'm needed, or how indispensable I am. I hope Mom now knows that I'm okay, that I'm not alone, because there is someone greater than me who has my back. But I also hope she knows that we miss seeing her sitting in her chair, that we miss her presence, and that her value to us was never in her doing, but in her "being."

CHAPTER 7

What We've Learned

As the dust clears and time passes, we are able to see things more clearly and objectively. While we are in the middle of the chaos, as with many of life's challenges, we are focused on surviving and putting out the fires as they come. We realize now that we were learning along the way and now are able to put things in perspective for ourselves and, we hope, for others.

Watching and helping someone prepare to leave this world and enter the next is terrifying. The changes they face both physically and mentally leave us feeling totally inadequate. We've learned that when the time comes, it will be a mixture of sadness and relief.

No matter how much you've talked, planned, and discussed these ends, you can never imagine every scenario. The caregiving responsibility is unlike anything you've ever faced. We are woefully naïve when it comes to taking medical, financial, and life and death decisions from our parents' hands and still leaving them with their dignity

It is everyone's desire to remain independent for as long as possible. The factors that play into that independence are often misconstrued. First and foremost is safety. However, independence does not mean merely living on your own. Independence doesn't mean relying on your children or family to do all your grocery shopping and transporting you to all your appointments. Independence means learning to seek out services that support you living on your own. Society offers many services that support the elderly in their homes. For example, Medicab may be available in many locations for getting to appointments, and some supermarkets and pharmacies deliver. Seniors can bank online on their own. In spite of all these services, some elderly prefer to depend on their children, because doing so is familiar and easiest on them. Depending solely on family members for your everyday needs stretches the resiliency of your family to a breaking point. The parent truly does not realize the impact all the caregiving has on the family.

Parents want an "exclusive" on our attention. They have typically been retired for some time and have lost track of demands of family and careers. They are not jealous of the relationships in our lives but resent the time those relationships take away from them. How difficult it must be for them to have gone from an active participant to an observer!

Life is just happening for them, and their world is becoming smaller. They can't see how they played any part in some of their unhappiness.

Some elders begin to rely solely on their children and slow-ly relinquish their friendships. Others depend solely on the opinions of friends. Unfortunately in this scenario the friends' judgment is not any more reliable than their own.

It almost resembles peer pressure like teenagers. We all know the battle that peer pressure could turn into.

When the physical and mental needs become more compli-cated, those peers step back, knowing it is beyond them, and the family must pick up the pieces once again. The parents are unhappy because all the relationships are changing and they've lost the ability to find happiness from within. They are expect-ing everyone to make them happy, but they have to play a part in their own happiness.

What is really happening and they don't realize it is not that the relationships are necessarily changing, but that their abil-ity to communicate is diminishing. That logical progression of thinking becomes secondary to defiance and getting their own way. We found parents will sometimes go to dangerous ex-tremes to get what they want, not unlike a rebellious teenager. How difficult it must be to take direction from your children when you can't recognize the danger in your behavior!

No matter how the aging and dying process advances and no matter how hard the caregiver has tried to make the time comfortable and leave the person with dignity, it is inevitable that the caregiver will be judged. You will be judged not only by family and friends but even by the person to whom you gave the care. We have learned and now try very hard not to be judgmental of others in similar situations.

The judgment passed may come across through insensitive words or at times no words at all but just a cold silence. Hang on to the kind words of compassion and understanding that you are given from those who know your heart and soul. Be strong when the negative judgment comes your way. Some people don't and really can't quite understand, since they have not truly lived it. When Catherine decided to move to senior housing, one individual actually jested that Louise threw her out. Nothing was further from the truth or more hurtful. It must be noted that this individual was much younger and couldn't fathom how difficult the situation could be.

Another daughter who lived quite a distance from her parents who were in a nursing home would visit once or twice a year yet felt it fine to share endless advice. A friend of Catherine's thought her daughter was terrible for allowing her to move out. Sadly that same friend now lives alone, cared for by strangers and visited by her daughter a few times a year. Her painful disappointment is written all over her face as any hope she had of being cared for by her daughter is gone.

Most critics do not know all of the heartbreaking details and perhaps have heard only a part of the story. Their words of judgment hurt.

We have learned that there are many caregivers facing a variety of issues. The issues are as individual and different as there are personalities and fingerprints. We share two stories. Martha withdrew and became completely dependent upon her daughter, Ann. Catherine became rebellious and defiant of any boundaries that would make her dependent upon Louise. Ann was smothered by Martha's dependence, and Louise was chasing a runaway freight train; therefore, it seems impossible to rely on any one set of guidelines for help.

Everyone is built differently, and we can't possibly know their story. There are many factors that go into family dynamics, and circumstances will most likely determine who will be the care-giver, often with no prior training, discussion, or commitment. The history of relationships can influence whether a person can or can't help. Even within the same household, one sibling may not be privy to relationship challenges faced by another sibling.

We've learned to accept the things we truly cannot change. Knowing the difference between what can be changed and what can't, however, is the cloudy part.

We can tell you all that our individual circumstances presented. There is no true guide for how difficult it is for the person pre-paring to leave this world and for those of us trying to support that person. There will be many people ready to move on to their next home, but there are just as many who want to hold on to the world they know. In the end no matter how much people love you and support you, it is a journey you take alone.

There is a confusion and unfairness when comparing illnesses of the body to the illness or fading of one's mind. Most physical illnesses, such as cancer, show the ravaged wounds and pain. Under the circumstances, somehow understanding and pa-tience are easier to find. As a mind fades, it is well hidden and begins with only hints. Understanding and patience is super-seded by confusion and frustration for both parties.

We've learned that there are doctors and nurses who go far beyond their call of duty to care for their elderly patients. They take the extra steps for the safety and well-being of those patients and their families. The elderly patient is not invisible to them. On the contrary, they see and consider the total person inside and out.

We've learned to look now at other caregivers of the elderly with a higher sense of understanding, compassion, and love, and we offer to just listen.

We have learned the importance of surrounding yourself with professionals and those who love you. There may not be an easy solution to your role as a caregiver, so you can do nothing more than ride out the storm.

In years to come, we may not remember all of that we went through, but we hope this book will help guide our own children and give them some permission to make decisions for us if necessary and to understand us and the new feelings of the new relationship we all may have. Most of all we hope they will understand and forgive themselves for not being perfect, because that's okay. For heaven's sake never take it personally!

As time goes by, the difficult years of caregiving fade, and again warm and wonderful memories shine brightly. The only thing still perfect is the deep love we have for our moms.

CHAPTER 8

Healing – *It Was Never Personal*

The familiar phrase "accept the things you cannot change" is easier said than done. We devoted so much time, love, and energy to our loved ones in caring for them, with endless hope of some change for the better, some improvement. The change for the better does not happen. It cannot happen, and we struggle to accept that. Our love keeps us holding on to hope, which makes it difficult to accept what we really can't change, so we continue caring forever, even after we lose our parent. Such a deep bond and a deep love makes it more difficult to see the reality. One would hope that love could conquer all, but it cannot. What this love does is give us the desire to help and hold on until the situation does not let us hold on any longer. We are forced to let go one way or another. We did not let go until God decided it was time. Even then, we let go of our loved one physically first. Emotionally we never really let go. That is our gift. Eventually we let go of the frustration as time goes on. The warm memories of happiness and humor live on forever.

One really must try to understand and convince oneself that it is not personal and it never was. Yes, our parent is resentful of us. Gently stepping in to help and trying not to let them feel we are taking control is very hard. They really do become difficult, as much as it hurts us also. They too are feeling a different kind of frustration, anger, and hurt. They are the ones losing some control, which must be emotionally devastating for them. They truly do not understand why. They are strong and stubborn and refuse to give up or give in. This strength and stubbornness helped them through the hardest times in their lives, and as they age, it is almost working against them. They never gave up or quit in life. We ask ourselves if we would want them to give up. Giving up seems worse. They would be empty and sad. There doesn't seem to be a better way, so it is not personal. It is not you they hate. They hate what is happening to them, but they can't help themselves.

We don't really think they realize what is happening to them. Can you imagine the fear inside them, holding on to every last bit of independence? Looking back, we see that our moms loved us as they always had. We, however, were their children, and they probably felt defeated facing the thought that a child was seeming to take charge. No matter how gently and carefully we tried to help, it was interpreted as controlling. Again, looking back, it is much easier to understand this. It was so hard to find the right words to hope our moms would realize we wanted to help, just help.

After ten years for Louise and five years for Ann, it didn't end with death. Our emotions kept reeling in more directions trying to understand and convince ourselves that we did the best we could. This "best" for our moms was added to everyday life holding our families, careers, and ourselves together. We are seeing friends trying to hold it all together, and now we are reaching out, listening, and consoling them. Just to tell someone you know how they feel, you know what they are going through, and you are here to listen any time, any day, helps you as much as it helps the caregiver. We now are being validated and understood. We also have a clearer understanding of ourselves. Many of the issues caregivers face are similar to the ones we faced. The one common denominator is feelings.

We spent many days and nights searching for reassurance from our families and friends. Please, someone, tell us we did a good job, but tell us so that we truly believe it. Believing we did well does finally come, but it takes time, time as in years. We both received the love and reassurance that we did the best for our moms. This reassurance first came from our families, friends, and each other, and now from seeing others face the task of caregiver. These things all helped mend our hearts and souls. Our problem was we couldn't convince ourselves that we were doing a good job. We were harder on ourselves than we should have been. Looking around now, we know we did good. Continued support from our friends and family made it easier, but as time went on and we met others experiencing the same situation and feelings, we finally saw the whole picture. Only then did we finally understand and know we did okay.

Although we had great emotional support, the day-to-day work was done by us, alone. It was more demanding than we ever imagined. We had to watch and listen for signs of problems 24/7. After all surgeries, we nursed them back to health. The more confused the parents became, the more we were the counselor or psychologist to console them. We took them to the doctors, dentists, malls, and supermarkets. It was a full-time job in addition to our other full-time jobs. We became their everything. Every day we prayed to be stronger and keep patient. Our faith and prayers gave us more strength. Exhaustion overwhelmed us at night, but sleep was too restless to catch up, so we continued without catching up.

As Ann and Louise had their long distance phone calls, they would talk about what Ann was encountering, and Louise understood and felt for her. Ann's words and feelings helped Louise find closure. Ann was saying and feeling exactly what Louise had felt many years earlier, so it was okay to be sad, frustrated, hurt, or angry. It was not personal for our moms nor was it personal for us. Our moms did not grow difficult on purpose. They were in an aging process that we were in the middle of now and each day. It was on the job training to the max! By listening to Ann, Louise was able to understand, finally. Now Ann and Louise each have listened to others and have felt for them and hoped to share some consolation. Not only do we listen, but we also hear them.

We hear the exhaustion, the hurt, and the frustration they are feeling. We hear and understand the awful feelings of helplessness.

We sincerely and candidly share our times of giving care and feeling the same. We realize now the sad silence was easier than any confrontation at all. For the first time in our lives we realized that the hope of having a truly logical conversation with our parent was fading fast.

We smile more some days now and ignore what was not all that important to worry about. We had many good days. When we look back, we realize our moms did not see or feel all of what we felt. That was good. We would hate ourselves if we hurt their feelings in any way. We are sure they felt the times of silence and may or may not have known why. We put up a good front, for them and for others. But at night, alone, we cried for some help. We just didn't know what kind of help. We did not want to lose our parents, but how long could we be strong enough, patient enough?

As we said, our healing did not start until after the loss of our moms. It came gradually with the love and support of family and friends.

Finally, having a friend with this in common made it clear to see, feel, and understand it all. A good friend, a good person, a spiritual person, and a loving person who could feel the same gave us validation. It was normal to wear down. We helped each other understand and find closure. We hope others can see more clearly that being a caregiver is one of the most difficult tasks but a task we would let no other do for us.

We would do it all over again, because we can love and smile sincerely now and understand.

Find your personal healing with professionals, clergy, family, friends, and others dealing with caring for a parent. It will take a long time to smooth out the wrinkled world you have been such a part of. It will become clearer with time and tears.

CHAPTER 9

Faith, The Ultimate Healer

Throughout our story we seem always to be referring to some-thing within us that could not see an option other than saying yes to caring for our moms. It is what our parents modeled; it was what our grandparents modeled. It is also a core value of our Christian tradition. We were not overly religious. Our families never preached religion; they lived it. They were far from perfect. That was part of the beauty. They never pretend-ed they had all the answers. We lived in a blue collar, faith-filled neighborhood. People struggled and didn't hide their troubles. We were lucky; we grew up seeing that life has challenges, but we also watched how neighbors helped neighbors and shared the good times and the hard times, how they ultimately trusted it would all work out.

That upbringing, that core faith, was such a huge part of who we were and are that it is what made us unable to say no. It was also the continuing of a lifelong conversion. It would lead to the challenges that would force us to look for something bigger than us, something beautiful in the midst of the storm. Each struggle would eventually bring us to the point of seeking a more intimate relationship with the God we were raised to trust. And it was our parents who started us on this lifelong journey.

In spite of a deep faith and a well-developed sense of who we were in Christ and what we were called to do, though, we fell short—at least in our eyes we did. The guilt was so strong that we found it difficult to find that God we so diligently sought. How could we be so angry and frustrated with the women who had always been there for us? These were the last days we would have with them, yet we couldn't find the beauty. They had given to us unconditionally their entire lives; when they needed us the most we did the best we could do.

We discovered that we spent a lot of our lives avoiding confrontation and trying to make those around us happy. Another tenet of our faith is service. We were raised to be servants. It is what we believe we are called to be. Somewhere along the line, however, our self-identity was defined by pleasing those around us instead of pleasing God. Sometimes it is difficult to separate the two. Surely we are expected to watch out for our fellow man, and surely that pleases God. But when your self-esteem comes from how happy you can make people, that's a co-dependency on each other instead of God. Our relationships had somehow become false idols. We idolized our mothers and our relationship with them. Being humbled is a painful experience, and our end days with our moms was indeed a humbling experience.

Much of our guilt comes from not being able to fulfill our mother's needs. We were self-reliant instead of being God reliant. We, as well as our mothers, forgot that God fulfills the needs.

We are merely His instrument. We were all guilty of relying on each other without consciously putting God in the middle as our anchor.

During those years of caregiving, we were hanging on by our fingertips. We were so exhausted and frustrated over los-ing the relationship that we idolized that we couldn't see the forest through the trees. In reality, the relationship was our identity. To lose it was to lose ourselves, so we hung on, and in the end, no matter how you slice it, we did it. We obeyed God and did what He wanted us to do, and through it all it was this core that got us up each day to try one more time, and for that, we believe we pleased Him.

Now that the dust is clearing, it is becoming more apparent that while we did what we were asked to do, we had to die to self and give material things—whether money, cars, prestige, or relationships—their proper place in our life. We chuckle because we sure thought we were dying to self during those years. In many ways we were but we still had a long way to go.

During this lost time we thought God had asked us to care give and then left us. Actually it was a time in the desert, a time to miss Him as our constant companion, a time to un-derstand that our moms couldn't fill that void, and perhaps a time for our mothers to understand that we couldn't fill their void either.

Perhaps taking care of our mothers was God's way of weaning us from our earthly parent. We were able to see each other's humanness and fall off the pedestals we had relegated each other to. We were human. We did our best to be as perfectly human and responsible and responsive as possible, but in reality, we were just human. We all did the best we could, and in the end it became time to forgive ourselves. We can stop trying to be the perfect mother, wife, child, sister, grandmother. We can rejoice in being a child of our most high God; beautifully and wonderfully made. We can know that it is He, not us, who will get us through each struggle to come.

It is this knowledge that helps us smile now. We can see the beauty in those long, endless days. We did do a good job. It wasn't doing it perfectly that was important; it was being obedient and being willing to try. Do we wish we were more spiritually mature so that our caregiving was done with more grace and joy? You bet. But like all challenges along life's journey, it is one more lesson under our belt. With each storm we often emerge with what we believe are all the tools and lessons needed to meet the next struggle. We suspect that our next chaotic time will be full of new lessons, but we are hopeful that we will have more tools in our toolbox.

As we seek to balance worldly needs with God's needs, we are careful not to create another false idol and not get caught up in the expectations of society. If we do, that noise keeps us from hearing His truth. It is the stillness that we seek, for it is there that we truly hear.

Our stillness is returning. We've stepped back from many of the things that feed our ego and self-image, but the beauty of submitting is the power of communication through prayer. Often our grandchildren are all talking at once, and our response is, "one child at a time". You can't hear when everyone is talking; listen for the answer. Imagine how God feels when we are always asking, begging, telling, demanding; the answer is in the silence, in being still.

We wish we could say we have arrived. We have done our best to learn from what we have experienced. We know there will be a next time. We only hope that we will be able to draw on what we have learned, that we will be able to embrace it with more grace and joy, that we will be able to die to self, see the beauty and opportunity in the journey, and trust Who is truly in charge.

We are not theologians any more than we are psychologists. I suspect practitioners of either of those professions could look at us and point to textbooks that confirm or deny much of what we say. However, our goal is to figure out what made us tick and how we are to come out of this experience stronger and wiser than when we went in. We are not textbooks; we are people who lived the experience and want to share the struggle from that perspective and most importantly, give praise to God—the One who gives us the truth—and bring our share of the talents He's given us to the world and have the strength and the grace to persevere and come into closer relationship with Him.

CPSIA information can be obtained
at www.ICGtesting.com
Printed in the USA
LVHW04s1717160718
583927LV00002B/269/P

9 781432 798703